We don't choose our parents—or the pain that they sometimes inflict. However, as adults we are free to seek healing and health. For those who are seeking, Drs. Beverly and Tom Rodgers point the way. I highly recommend *Becoming a Family that Heals*.

> Gary D. Chapman, Ph.D.
> Author of *The Five Love Languages* and *Love As a Way of Life*

For me, the most important treasure in life is my family—and keeping it together is tough. That's because relationships take work. We are broken in relationships—and healed in relationships. The great paradox is that if there's brokenness in your family, the path to healing is found in those very relationships along with the wonderful work that God is doing to get you beyond the pain to a new and better life! In their book, *Becoming a Family that Heals*, Drs. Tom and Beverly Rodgers lay out a path of healing to protect your greatest treasure!

> Dr. Tim Clinton, LPC, LMFT
> Author, licensed counselor, and president of the 50,000 member American Association of Christian Counselors

Every family, no matter how healthy, needs healing. And Tom and Beverly's book is sure to be a catalyst for helping you heal the hurts that might otherwise fragment your bonds.

> Drs. Les and Leslie Parrott
> Founders of RealRelationships.cc

D1531382

Today's families are besieged with pressures and negative influences like never before in our history. To add to their stress, parents often unknowingly carry baggage from their pasts into their family relationships, causing a great many problems. The Rodgers's book offers readers solid, tried-and-true techniques for resolving those issues and healing these troubled families. Written in a very conversational, readable style, this book brings hope and healing to every family who will have the courage to read its pages. We enthusiastically endorse both the writing and the work of Drs. Beverly and Tom Rodgers.

Claudia and David Arp
Authors of *10 Great Dates* and *Fixing Family Friction*

Drs. Beverly and Tom Rodgers not only offer a candid look into the journey of how one couple's marriage and family was healed, but through their tasteful transparency as licensed counselors we also get to follow their own "soul-healing" journey as well. Thank you, Beverly and Tom, for a much-needed book that speaks to both ends of the spectrum!

Joe and Michelle Williams
Authors of *Yes, Your Marriage Can Be Saved*

Becoming a Family
that Heals

HOW TO RESOLVE PAST ISSUES

AND FREE YOUR FUTURE

Drs. Beverly and Tom Rodgers

 Tyndale House Publishers, Inc., Carol Stream, Illinois

Library of Congress Cataloging-in-Publication Data
Rodgers, Beverly, 1954-
  Becoming a family that heals / Beverly Rodgers and Tom Rodgers.
    p. cm.
  "A Focus on the Family book"—T.p. verso.
  Includes bibliographical references.
  ISBN 978-1-58997-575-0
  1. Family—Religious aspects—Christianity. 2. Psychology, Religious.
I. Rodgers, Tom, 1950- II. Title.
  BV4526.3.R63 2009
  248.4—dc22
                                        2009009029

Printed in the United States of America
1 2 3 4 5 6 7 8 9 / 15 14 13 12 11 10 09

Contents

Acknowledgments

So many of the great Christian authors whose works we read dedicate their books to their parents or acknowledge their parents' contribution to their life's work. We have so often commented upon how great this would be for us. But for reasons you will discover in this book, you will see that this isn't the case for us. We can, however, express overwhelming gratitude to our heavenly Father who has stood in the gap when we felt like emotional orphans and showed up every day at our computer to help us pen this manuscript. Thank you, Abba, again and again.

We are grateful to our clinic staff at Rodgers Christian Counseling and the Institute for Soul Healing Love who make it a joy to go to work every day and walk shoulder-to-shoulder with us in helping hurting families. Their belief and camaraderie take the stress out of hearing people pour out their pain for hours at a time. We are honored by the thousands of hurting souls who, over the past three decades, have trusted us with their pain. This book is our gift to you.

We cannot express enough appreciation for our editor, Kathy Davis, whose keen eye and editorial wisdom took our jumbled thoughts and transformed them into very readable prose. Thanks to the rest of the team at Focus on the Family—Cami Heaps, Shari Martin, Josh Shepherd, and Larry Weeden—for their belief in the work that God has called us to do.

Lastly, words cannot express enough gratitude to our daughters Amanda and Nicole for their patience and long-suffering as we attempted to build a healthy family from the ruins that were our childhoods. Thank you for honoring us and teaching us.

Meet the Smith Family

s the sun set over the trees behind our office, it cast an amber glow over Amy Smith's face, making her look tired and sad as she poured out her heart. In her expressive, emotional style she shared about her 15-year marriage. Her husband, Bill, sat uncomfortably stiff on the far side of the sofa, his arms crossed in a resistant, nervous posture.

Amy told us that they had two beautiful children, Chloe, age eight, and Billy, six. Amy began to cry as she revealed that she was at her wits' end with Bill because he would not interact with her and the children. He spent most of his evenings and weekends parked in front of the television in his room, or "dungeon," as they called it.

"He won't talk or relate to us. He just works and comes home and disappears into his room," she shared through her tears. "Chloe will do anything to get his attention. She even tried to be interested in fishing so she could spend time with him. But he just won't respond to her. This kills me because I know how she feels. I tried to get my dad's attention when I was her age, and when I could not reach him, it caused me to rebel and become promiscuous. There's so much to deal with here," Amy cried, wiping her tears in embarrassment.

"Our marriage is in trouble," she continued. "Our son is having behavior problems at school, and poor Chloe has ADHD and has trouble with her school work. She has no friends because her self-esteem is on the floor. The problems in our family seem so big that I just don't know where to start. I finally told Bill that if he did not come to counseling I might have to leave. I still can't believe he came today," she said as she looked at him for some type of reaction. But Bill just stared blankly at Amy, in what appeared to be his typical shutdown response. This just made Amy cry even harder. The hopelessness and despair in the room were palpable.

As Christian marital and family therapists for the past 28 years, we have treated many families like the Smiths. These families are typically desperate and overwhelmed, and they need help on many fronts. It is our job to help them eat the proverbial elephant of healing family dysfunction, one bite at a time. Often, when people are inundated with problems, they cannot see a way out. But there is hope for this family and many others like them. Tom and I found that same hope for our own wounded family years ago.

Yes, we too have had problems. Just because we're marriage and family counselors does not mean that we're immune to trouble. We too came from homes where there was a great deal of pain. My mother was mentally ill. She was abusive to our family, both mentally and physically. As you can imagine, it caused a great deal of stress on my parents' marriage. My father finally left my family when I was five years old. This exacerbated my mother's illness and she became even more angry and abusive. It was difficult growing up without a dad and many times without a mother; mentally ill moms are frequently missing in action. It was not until I started college and studied psychology that I realized the full impact my wounded childhood would have on my life and my marriage.

Tom grew up in a seemingly more "normal" family—at least no one was crazy! Even so, his family had troubles of its own. They were churchgoers and were there every time the doors were open. They were considered pillars of their small community in central California. Everything ran smoothly for them until Tom's father's repeated adultery was exposed.

Tom's whole world came crashing down then, and this started the slow and painful dissolution of his family. They had to move from their community in shame and nothing was the same after that.

Tom entered college with a poor ability to trust because everything that he put his trust in had disintegrated. His parents finally buried their dead, dysfunctional marriage when Tom was 25 years old. Though he was an adult when his parents eventually divorced, the hurt was no less painful. Like most Christian children of divorce, he even doubted God. All of this followed him into our marriage.

We were much like Amy and Bill Smith. We had no idea that we brought wounds from our respective families into our marriage. We now believe it was because of these wounds that we became therapists. It was because of our hurt and pain that we eventually developed a model for healing relationships. We call it the Soul-Healing Love Model. You'll be hearing a lot about how it can work in your life as we follow the Smith family in their healing process. Along with the Smiths, you will learn how your childhood wounds have affected your adult relationships, and how to apply the soul healing balm of the Great Physician to these wounds so that you can have healthy, lasting family relationships.

SOUL-HEALING LOVE

We never started out to develop a counseling model. If you had known us in college, you would have assumed that we were the least likely candidates to do so. We were so insecure and fearful of trusting one another. We entered our relationship with so many wounds that we spent the first year of our marriage in a counselor's office. We studied family interaction in school, attended workshops, read as many books as we possibly could, studied Scripture, and prayed often. Still, marriage was hard.

It wasn't easy to attend classes and seminars by great Christian leaders who seemed to have it all together. We thought our childhood wounds would disqualify us from ever being able to help ourselves, much less anyone else. In the early years of our training it seemed incongruous for us to study about creating healthy families while our own family fell miserably short. We felt hypocritical when we would help a family stop their unhealthy patterns, only to repeat our own later on. It took a while to learn that all leaders feel this struggle in some way or another as they try to live out what they teach.

The Lord was good and heard our cries, and in time gave us ways to heal our wounded marriage and pass this healing on to others. This became the Soul-Healing Love Model. It integrates psychological principles and biblical truths so that couples and families can understand each other better, gain insight into their own and each other's woundedness, have empathy for one another, move toward forgiveness, and become healing agents to each other. The premise of the model is that God's unconditional love heals our wounded souls and restores us to wholeness. Jeremiah 30:17 says, " 'But I will restore you to health and heal your wounds,' declares the Lord." As we experience God's great soul-healing love, we can allow that love to overflow to our family, so that we can be healing agents to them as well. Because loving your family can be harder at times than loving your neighbors, the Lord gave us practical, doable ways to walk out God's unconditional love. It is nothing short of miraculous how the Lord can take a fearful, fractured family and move it to a healing place. We now use the model in our large counseling clinic in Charlotte, North Carolina, and travel the globe doing workshops and teaching other counselors and pastors how to use it.

As you can see, the Lord used our pain to help us be an example to others, so we now believe that God does not waste pain. He did not waste ours, and we knew He would use the pain of the Smith family for good as well. Now, let's accompany the Smiths on their healing journey and see how the Soul-Healing Love concepts worked for them, and more importantly, how they can work for you and your family.

Chapter One

In the Beginning: Wounded People Marry Wounded People and Wound Children

*I*n order to deal with Bill and Amy's obvious pain, we wanted to let them know that they were not alone in their struggles, that many couples have difficulties like theirs, and that their family could be healed. Watching their mixture of relief and skepticism as we shared, we moved on to asking them the all-important question: "What do you two want out of counseling?"

Amy had a list and was ready, almost anxious, to share it. We could tell that she had been preparing for this session for some time. Of course, the list contained everything she wanted to change about Bill, but there was no mention of anything she needed to improve. (We would have to deal with this later.)

"I want Bill to talk to me more, to interact with the kids more, to get involved in their projects, and help around the house." She was on a roll by now and we could see where this was going, but could not even break in to slow her down. Bill, obviously feeling put down, sat lower and lower on the sofa until the cushions enveloped him. We could tell he was clenching his teeth as he rolled his eyes in utter frustration.

Oblivious to Bill's mood, Amy continued to lament. "I want Bill to tell me what's going on in his brain. He shuts me out so much! I want him to be a spiritual leader and care about how our children are doing spiritually." She finally took a breath long enough for me to get a word in.

We knew we needed to get Bill to talk before he exploded, so I asked, "What about you, Bill? What brought you here today?"

"She did, she made me come," he said somewhat sarcastically. (We soon learned that this playful sarcasm was Bill's communication trademark.)

"I hate this sort of thing. I can't stand sharing feelings anyway, much less with strangers. No offense to you guys, but talking about emotions is like torture for me."

"Most of us guys have trouble with this," Tom replied in an effort to comfort and identify with Bill. "In fact, after thirty-two years of marriage, my wife is still teaching me new ways to share feelings, so we hope we can make this as painless as possible for you."

"Wow, thirty-two years and you seem okay . . . well sort of," Bill replied with that same hint of sarcastic humor. We all chuckled and it seemed to lighten up the serious mood.

Finally, Tom asked, "So, Bill, why are you *really* here?"

"Well, if you really want to know, my biggest complaint is about Amy's nagging. She always tells me what I'm not doing. No matter what I do, it is never enough for her. I finally just quit trying because there is no pleasing her."

"Bill was not always so shut down," Amy interrupted. (We were also soon to learn that this was her trademark communication style.) "He talked all the time when we dated. I think he tricked me into marrying him, and after he finally caught me, his sullen self appeared," she said resentfully.

"You'd be sullen too if you lived with her constant nagging," Bill defended himself. "She thinks she's right about everything. It's too bad we all can't be perfect like her," he added somewhat scornfully.

"I don't want perfection, I just want someone who is more involved with the family, like I am. Why can't Bill be more like me?" she asked.

"I have wondered the same thing," Bill said. "How did I pick a wife who is so different from me?"

Tom and I have been asked this question by couples thousands of times in the last three decades. The problem is that people are typically not attracted to mates who are similar to themselves. As with countless couples we see in our office, Bill and Amy could hardly be more opposite. Amy was verbal, expressive, and animated, with a great vocabulary and no problem using it. Bill was her opposite: quiet, stoic, and emotionally frozen.

We have found that we may date individuals more like ourselves, but when it comes to selecting a mate, we typically pick our opposite. This is because, as the old saying goes, opposites attract. There are actually physiological, psychological, and spiritual reasons for this. So to help them see that their differences could actually be a good thing, we explained to Bill and Amy what we are about to share with you.

OPPOSITES ATTRACT

For years relationship researchers have known that people are attracted to partners who are their opposite, but the issue of opposites attracting really goes back to the Garden of Eden. God, the Creator of the universe, has male and female characteristics, masculine and feminine. God made man in His image (Genesis 1:26). Adam reflected the male aspect of His image. He was put on the earth to do God's masculine tasks. He was to protect, serve, and have charge over all of God's creatures (Genesis 1:26–27).

In those first days, Adam was busy with his charge. He was responsible for naming all living things. As he did this, he utilized all of his, and God's, masculine qualities. But it wasn't long before he realized that something was missing. As God's male image bearer, Adam permeated and interacted with the creation, but God's feminine image was noticeably absent. The world needed His feminine characteristics.

Adam needed God's feminine side too. When God said that it was not good for man to be alone (Genesis 2:18), He wanted Adam to have this part of His likeness to complete His creation. Adam needed his opposite to feel complete and to be able to experience and utilize all of God's aspects and characteristics, and husbands and wives have been looking for that completeness with each other ever since.

DIVINE ONENESS

When man (God's male likeness) craves woman (God's female likeness) they marry and become *one.* In this oneness, they fulfill a divine destiny. Webster's gives one definition of *destiny* as "set apart for a specific purpose." Since couples have both parts of God's nature, they can do so much more together than they could alone to fulfill their special purpose. Together they form what we call the "Divine Us." This Us is greater than the sum of the two parts.

Now, don't misunderstand. We are not saying here that we as humans are divine. Far from it! Rather, the Divine Us is a calling that God has for only a specific couple, *that* man and *that* woman in all of their uniqueness, with the qualities that only those two people possess. Together they can learn to transcend their differences, even learn from these dissimilarities, and grow to be all that God has called them to be. God has a plan for the Divine Us that can be accomplished only when the two become one.

Tom and I have worked hard over the years to determine and develop our Divine Us. We have often said that without each other there are many things we simply would not, or could not, do. We're certain that separately we would not have started a counseling, writing, and speaking ministry. Together we gave each other courage to do the things we would not do alone. I am gifted in administration. This is an area where Tom is lacking. Tom has a great sense of direction, both literally (I get lost in every hotel we stay in), and figuratively, in that he often knows the path that we should take in life.

These are not the only areas where Tom and I are opposites. I am very outgoing; he has a shy streak. I'm hyper and can't sit still. He is far calmer. He's athletic. I'm uncoordinated! Like our couple Amy and Bill, I am a talker, and Tom is a man of few words. More than once in our marriage these opposite characteristics have caused us conflict. On more than one occasion, I have wished for a mate who was more like me. Yet, before we met I had dated guys who were more like me, and I found that there wasn't a great deal of attraction. I even found some to be boring. We just didn't have chemistry.

CHEMISTRY AND LOVE

Relationship researchers report that the more opposite the couple, the greater the chemistry. In fact, the term *chemistry* came from the science of alchemy, a forerunner of modern chemistry. It was a mixture of science and philosophy that developed in the Middle Ages when people were attempting to find an elixir of life.[1] Early chemists knew that the more opposite the chemicals were, the greater the explosive reaction when they were mixed! Perhaps these early chemists saw the explosive reaction between opposite men and women as they declared undying love and devotion for each other.

There is also a biological reason for this chemistry. When you first fall in love, hormones and brain chemicals flow throughout your body.

Researchers at the University of New York call this "the love cocktail."[2] These chemicals cause us to feel superhuman, making the "in love" feelings soar. They also alter our thinking so that we see our partner in the most positive light. So while we are dating, we not only overlook the opposite characteristics in our prospective mates, we actually like those very characteristics!

When we dated, I loved that Tom was laid-back and could take breaks when we studied. He loved it that I was driven and could accomplish a great deal in a short time. He got more done when he was with me, and I could relax more in his presence. It was not long after we married that those blessed brain chemicals began to fade, and our differences started to annoy us.

"Can't you sit still?" he would ask.

"Are you taking another break? We have work to do," I would bemoan.

The differences that we once celebrated and enjoyed soon became grist for the mill of marital conflict. Take a moment and think about the main thing that you were attracted to in your mate. Do you fight about this issue today? You will understand more about this as you read through the pages of this book. But first, let's look at another way husbands and wives can be opposites.

SIMILAR WOUNDS/OPPOSITE ADAPTATIONS

Not only do opposite personalities attract, but people with opposite adaptations to similar wounds attract as well. This is the basis for dysfunctional family systems. Harville Hendrix in his book *Keeping the Love You Find*, says that we are attracted to people who have similar wounds from the past. It is not that we consciously know that people have similar wounds. Of course, we don't ask about one's childhood wounds on the first date, but we do find that there is just something about that person that feels familiar. Hendrix calls this "the phenomenon of recognition."[3] This causes us to feel at home with people who have had similar experiences. In our counseling we have found that adult children of alcoholics find other adult children of alcoholics. Children of divorce find other children of divorce. Those who are abused as children may find mates who will abuse them. Though it seems crazy to outsiders, it feels familiar and comfortable to the ones inside the relationship.

This "phenomenon of recognition" was the case with us. Tom and I attended a Christian university in the 1970s. Most of the students came from wonderful Christian homes with great Christian heritages. We were two of only a handful of students who suffered from the divorces of our parents. And yet, among thousands of students, we managed to find each other. The chemistry between us was so potent that all of our friends noticed it immediately. Indeed, people with similar wounds are attracted to one another.

The problem is that though people may have similar wounds, they may also have opposite ways of dealing with those wounds. We call those ways *adaptations*. Tom adapted to his parents' painful divorce by withdrawing and isolating, becoming a loner. When my family fell apart I felt abandoned. I adapted to this wound by taking care of everyone and trying to fix things. I became a caretaker.

Here's how that worked out in our marriage. When we had conflict, I typically fell into my caretaking adaptation. I pestered Tom to respond, often following him from room to room, trying to get him to open up to me so that I could "fix" the situation. This pursuing caused Tom to feel suffocated and pull away even more, which caused him to fall into his adaptation as a loner. The more he would withdraw, the more abandoned I felt. The more abandoned I felt, the more I pursued him and the more he would distance himself. We were in a crazy, vicious cycle and unwittingly became the classic pursuer/distancer dyad that John Gottman talks about in his book *The Marriage Clinic*.[4]

In the Soul-Healing Love Model we call this phenomenon Marital Pac-Man, where one mate chases the other, and the other runs in fear of being emotionally "chomped up." This is a common problem in marriage, and fortunately it can be repaired. To do this, though, we needed to stop our unhealthy adaptations. As a distancer, Tom needed to bite the bullet and move closer. As a pursuer, I needed to practice self-control and back off more. We learned to do this for each other by rediscovering and appreciating what we were attracted to in the beginning of our relationship. This enabled us to move toward becoming more like each other.

This was exactly what Bill and Amy Smith needed to do as well. But first we wanted to explore more about their history and how they got trapped in their unhealthy game of Marital Pac-Man.

Chapter Two

Bill and Amy's Stories

*T*he sun had now set and you could hear the famous southern katydids and crickets creating a symphony outside our office window. They appeared to have a calming effect on the Smiths. Amy and Bill had been talking for almost an hour and by now they both seemed more comfortable. As the darkness closed in outside, they shared a little of their past with us, and we explored how they got to this desperate place in their family.

AMY'S STORY

Amy told us that she grew up in a typical southern mill town. All of the people in the town worked at the mill and everyone knew everyone else. Her father was the mill supervisor, a position that carried a lot of weight and responsibility. He was at work all the time. When he was home, which was seldom, he was distant and hard to connect with. Amy dealt with this by doing everything she could to get him to notice her. She made good grades, received awards, cleaned the house, and kept out of trouble—all to no avail. Amy's dad died without giving her the blessing of his attention and affection. In many ways, she was still trying to get that blessing from Bill, and his silence was wounding her in much the same way that her dad had wounded her.

BILL'S STORY

Bill shared that his dad was a hard-driving alcoholic. He worked long hours as a steel worker and stopped off at the bar every night after work. "He frequently came home late and lit," was Bill's playfully sarcastic description. "If any one of us three kids got out of line, he would let us have it with the belt or the back of his hand. There were three boys in my house, so you can imagine how many times one of us incurred his wrath! None of us could please my dad and that is still true to this day."

Bill said that he dealt with his father's critical nature by withdrawing. He kept to himself and tried not to start trouble. In other words, he distanced, which was what he also did with Amy and the children.

We explained to Bill and Amy that they were enmeshed in the classic pursuer/distancer dyad. Amy hounded Bill for closeness and connection to heal her neglect wound from her father, and Bill ran away because closeness was so uncomfortable for him. When Amy's attempts to engage Bill were rebuffed by him, she would criticize him for being so distant. This criticism reminded Bill of his alcoholic father's rants. This was a trigger that caused him to withdraw even more, the way he did as a child. Amy and Bill were wounding each other in the same manner that they were hurt as children. It was easy to see why they were so miserable. In their woundedness, Bill and Amy often inadvertently hurt their own children as well.

THE CHILDREN'S STORY

Amy lamented, "I just know that the trouble in our relationship is affecting our kids. This just kills me. Billy's teacher called the other day and said that he got in trouble at school for fighting with another boy. I think that it's really all about the tension in our home. I try to fix Billy (not a surprise) by getting him to talk to me. Bill deals with it by yelling at Billy and punishing him. I'm afraid that Bill is following in his punitive dad's footsteps."

Once again, Bill wanted to speak, but Amy continued, trying to get everything she could out in the first session.

"Chloe cries at night when she says her prayers. She confided in me that she thinks her dad doesn't love her." Tears formed in the corners of Amy's eyes as she shared. Bill looked concerned, but defensive, as he rolled his eyes.

"Chloe spends the whole evening trying to get Bill's attention by making him coffee and asking for help with her homework," Amy continued. "But Bill just stays in his dungeon and defensively says that he provides a lot more for his kids than his distant father ever did for him." It was obvious to us that the fact that Bill could not see that he was hurting his children had caused Amy's resentment to grow even more.

"When I disagree with Bill's extreme punishments, he tells me that he is a great father compared to his alcoholic dad who would have beaten him for getting in trouble at school. I told him that he cannot compare himself to his abusive father. Just because you're not as bad as him doesn't mean that you have no need for improvement," Amy said, as her anger turned toward Bill.

Bill defended himself, "My kids are so lucky to have us. They have it made. They have no idea what a hard childhood really is."

"We understand that very well, Bill," Tom said with compassion. "We can see that you are a much better father than your abusive dad, but Amy is right. In fact, we have had to share this with many a parent in the last twenty-eight years. And this is important, so I want you to get it," Tom said, leaning forward even more for emphasis. "*Just because you aren't as bad as your parents, it does not mean that your parenting is healthy!*"

As with many parents who incorrectly compare themselves to

dysfunctional, abusive parents, this was hard for Bill to hear. So, just as we have done so many times before, we led Bill and Amy to the Word of God.

THE WISDOM OF A SAGE

We told the couple that it has often been said that the Bible is the greatest marriage manual of all time. After 32 years of marriage, that concept has become invaluable to us. Often when Tom and I need hope and direction from Scripture, we turn to the book of Isaiah. We have used this prophet's words as a beacon for our lives. Throughout this book we will unpack the words of this great scribe and show you how God had His hand on His family, Judah, in ancient times, and still has His hand on families today.

Bill and Amy listened as we turned to Isaiah 30:18–20 and Tom read, " 'Yet the Lord longs to be gracious to you; he rises to show you compassion. For the Lord is a God of justice. Blessed are all who wait for him!' The prophet goes on to tell us to weep no more. He will help you when you cry. Although He gives you the bread of adversity and the water of affliction, 'He will hear you.' "

"I have often felt that way and wondered why things have to be so hard," Amy commented.

"Me too!" Bill added.

"Many times Tom and I felt that we were given the bread of adversity and the water of affliction in our families of origin," I shared, "but the Lord did not forget us in our trouble, and He will not forget you. You have had a lot of adversity in your past and are facing a lot in the present, but the Lord can turn all of this around if you will only let Him." I then spent a few minutes sharing about some of our similar childhood experiences, in an effort to let them both know that we had been in their shoes and knew what they were feeling.

"The Lord has graciously heard us in the midst of our trials and afflictions and He will hear you," I assured them. "As you start the journey of soul healing, the Lord will have compassion on you and dry your tears and give you hope."

This appeared to minister to Amy, and we saw a softening in Bill's stoic countenance. We even heard a sigh of relief from him. This encouraged us to go deeper, so Tom and I knew that it was time to share Healing Premise #1 with this couple.

"Are you two ready for one more lesson before you go?" Tom asked.

They nodded their assent and we could see the mixture of relief and deep interest as Tom began to share.

HEALING PREMISE #1:
Opposites attract, and God intended this
to be a means of growth for couples.

"Just as God brought His maleness (man) and His femaleness (woman) together to grow them into marital oneness, He also brings two people who are opposites together to grow them as well. The shy guy marries the outgoing social butterfly and grows to be more comfortable in social situations. The risk-averse girl meets the risk-taking guy and becomes more daring because she is with him.

"When this happens, we are thrilled with a sense of completeness. We are also under the influence of the 'love cocktail' and are like two love-lost teenagers running from the opposite ends of a field just to jump into an embrace and become one. But as time wears on and brain chemicals wear off, we no longer run into each other's arms. In fact, these differences begin to grate on us, and instead of completeness we begin to feel uncomfortable. You wonder why your wife is so outgoing at parties."

Tom looked at Bill and then turned to Amy. "You question why your husband takes so many risks. That which you loved and appreciated becomes what you fight about in marriage. Instead of a warm embrace, you start chipping away at this oneness, sandpapering each other's differences. Why? Because they make you feel ill-at-ease, self-conscious, even less than who you should be because your partner has some quality that you lack.

"The differences that you once celebrated now challenge you too much," Tom continued. "You feel inadequate around your spouse, who is so opposite, and as a result you criticize him or her. Your partner then defends his or her behavior and becomes entrenched and refuses to change. By the time the cycle of criticism and defensiveness is set in motion, you end up in polarized positions and cannot see each other's perspective. You cannot really hear or communicate well with each other when this happens."

Both Amy and Bill were on the edge of their seats as they listened intently to this healing premise.

"This is exactly what happens to us!" Amy said, as the insight light bulb went off in her head. "It's as if you were a fly on the wall watching us interact at home! Don't you think so, Bill?"

"Yeah, spooky," he quipped. They shared with us that when they first met, Amy loved Bill's quiet, strong-silent-type demeanor. Bill loved it that Amy was so talkative. When they were dating they wanted to be more like each other.

I said, "The goal of your oneness should have been to develop a Divine Us, where Bill grew to talk more and become more able to connect, and Amy grew to listen more and fix less." I explained further that if they grew to become more like each other, they would soon be balanced. Bill, of course, would never be as talkative as Amy, but he would talk more. Amy would never be as quiet as Bill, but she would calm down and be able to rest more. That is God's purpose for the Divine Us; couples grow in areas where they are lacking. They move to be more like their mate, their opposite, so that they both can find balance.

Like Amy and Bill, couples fight about this Divine Oneness and in their defended state move further and further away from change. By the time we see them in counseling, they are poles apart, both thinking that they are right and that their partner is wrong.

THE SOLUTION

The way out for Amy and Bill and others like them is to stop resisting their differences, and start embracing them. We shared with the Smiths that the solution to this dilemma is recognizing that God gives us mates who are our opposite to *grow us*. This piqued their interest.

I continued, "Marriage is a crucible of growth to make us more balanced, so that we can be everything we need to be for God's kingdom. Bill and Amy, it is time to stop fighting over the ways that you are different. Stop criticizing each other because your mate is not more like you. Remember why you married each other in the first place. Recall how these differences changed you so long ago and can do so again. Surrender to this process. Instead of smacking up against each other, chipping off pieces of one another in a struggle to maintain too much autonomy, embrace this oneness. Don't fight it."

By this time, they were both nodding their heads in assent.

Tom then gave the Smiths some specific behavioral homework. We usually end each of our counseling sessions with homework and we will end various chapters of this book with what we call "Healing Homework" as well. Over the years, we have learned that this homework is important, not only in helping a family change the attitudes of the individuals within it, but it is also important for changing their behavior as well. We have a saying that if nothing changes, then nothing changes. Therefore, we wanted to make it practical for Bill and Amy to change their behavior as well as their perspective.

Tom instructed, "Bill, follow Amy's lead and talk more to her and the children. Spend at least fifteen minutes twice a week asking them questions. Take a walk with Amy at least once a week, and share a small part of your day; do what you did when you were dating and it wasn't so hard."

To make it easier for Bill, we asked Amy to talk less. She had to stop pleading, criticizing, and nagging Bill to get more involved; it wasn't working anyway! Amy had to be calmer and stop trying to fix things. She was to act more like she did when she first met Bill. In other words, act more like each other! They both agreed and stated that they felt hopeful and relieved after their first session and were not as afraid to come back for more. This awareness and acceptance was huge for a family like this one. It was a good start.

Now, what about you? Do you and your spouse need to discover your Divine Us? Here is your homework. As a couple you should both answer these questions and then discuss them.

HEALING HOMEWORK

~ What attracted you to your mate when you first met?
~ In many ways, is he or she your opposite?
~ Do you fight about those differences today?
~ How do you think the Lord wants you to grow to be more like your spouse in order to develop a Divine Us?
~ How can this be good for both of you?

Chapter Three

Where Did the Wounding Start?

*A*my entered the office more at ease this time as she took off her bright green jacket and laid it on the back of the sofa. Bill was still somewhat tentative, which is not uncommon for husbands who have been dragged into counseling by "helpful" wives.

"We had a better week," Amy said, as she plopped into the soft cushions on the sofa. They sat a little closer this time and Amy reached out several times to affectionately touch Bill when she spoke. "I read Isaiah chapter thirty several times last week. It really helped that you told us when we have the 'bread of adversity and the water of affliction,' that the Lord will comfort and help us."

Bill sat quietly next to Amy and peeped, "Yeah, it did help. And I was a good boy and sort of did my homework. I went on a walk with Amy and the kids," he said with only a slight hint of his usual sarcasm.

"How did that feel?" Tom asked.

"It was okay, but I realized that I'm not so good at asking them questions. I have a lot to learn."

"The important thing is that now he seems to want to learn," Amy added as she patted his shoulder. "Chloe was so excited that he was paying attention to her that she became hyper. As I told you, she suffers from ADHD," Amy reminded us. "Anyway, this got on Bill's nerves—

ed not to look at your family of origin is not un-

but at least he didn't yell at her like he has done in the past." Bill shrugged in assent to Amy's story, obviously grateful for her praise and affection.

FAMILY HISTORY

As we do with all of our clients, we asked Bill and Amy if we could get a family history. Tom grabbed a pen and turned to a fresh page on his note pad, and I began to ask questions. Amy had read our material and was prepared. We could tell that she had anticipated this moment for weeks. She moved to the edge of the sofa as she said, "I knew you would ask this and I think that it has everything to do with the way Bill is. You see, his father was a very mean alcoholic and ruled his family with an iron fist. His dad was verbally and physically abusive to Bill and his two brothers. If his mom tried to intervene, he would abuse her too. He's mellow now, but when those boys were little, he was a tyrant."

"Wait a minute," Bill said defensively, "Why are we dumping on my family? Your family is not that great either. Besides, I hate it when people blame all of their problems on their parents." Amy looked a little frustrated and confused.

"Bill, your reluctance to look at your family of origin is not uncommon. People often have a hard time seeing their parents in a negative light," Tom assured him. "But if you give this process a chance, it just might help you."

Over the years of working with people, we have seen that Bill's response is very typical. We have noticed that no matter how bad parents may be, children have a tendency to defend them. Tom has a saying: "Parents can be sacred cows. You may be starving to death, but you are not going to eat the cows." We explained to Bill that our goal was not to put our parents in a negative light or bring shame to them in any way. Many of them were wounded too, and they were simply living what they learned and inadvertently passing this on to us. In fact, we say in our Soul Healers Couples Weekends that "blame is not our game." We don't want to blame our parents for our past hurts; we simply want to acknowledge these hurts so that we can see how they affected us. We do this to recognize the results of those wounds in our lives, and to ask the Lord to heal them. If you don't know or accept what your wounds are, then you cannot move to heal them.

Bill continued to resist, leaning forward as he explained, "I just don't understand how something that happened thirty years ago could possibly have anything to do with what is happening to us today."

Once again, Bill was not alone in his common response. Many people become uncomfortable when we ask them to recall their painful pasts. They feel that if they ignore the past, then it will not bother them. Unfortunately, nothing could be further from the truth. In order to help Bill deal with his resistance to looking at past pain, we introduced Healing Premise #2.

HEALING PREMISE #2:
Whether you believe it or not, your childhood
does affect your adult relationships.

The things that have happened in our early lives can have a great effect on our conscious and unconscious minds. Typically we have little awareness of our subconscious, so if you ignore hurt and pain from the past, it has a way of coming back to haunt you. It can affect your health with headaches, upset stomachs, and other psychosomatic illnesses. Or it can affect your relationships as you treat people the way you have been treated. You may not be conscious that this is happening, but it is powerful nonetheless.

BRAIN FUNCTIONING AND SOUL WOUNDS

Have you ever wondered why you respond to certain situations in a particular way? Perhaps you overreact or become angry with your spouse and children, and like the apostle Paul, you do the very thing you hate. Paul said in Romans 7:19, "When I want to do good, I don't; and when I try not to do wrong, I do it anyway" (TLB). The NIV says, "What a wretched man I am! Who will rescue me from this body of death?" (Romans 7:24). Paul wasn't too far off in his questioning. The answer to our human dilemma lies in the body—in the brain to be exact.

For the sake of simplicity, let's imagine that when we are wounded in childhood, memories of these events form "wrinkles" on the brain, metaphorically speaking. The more traumatic the memory, the deeper the "wrinkle" or groove. Childhood traumatic memories make the deepest grooves of all, because the brain is still forming during this time. Tom and I call these painful memories soul wounds.

The interesting thing about soul wounds is that these traumatic memories are not recorded or stored in the frontal lobe, or neocortex, of the brain, but instead are stored in the cerebellum. The neocortex is the part of the brain that takes in information and draws rational conclusions about it. This is where reasoning, judgment, complex cognitive behaviors, decision making, self-evaluation, and moderation of correct social behavior occur. The neocortex allows us to observe ourselves doing things from an objective perspective.

The cerebellum, on the other hand, is called the old brain because it is the more rudimentary part of the brain and is very primitive in its functioning. It is the seat of primitive powerful emotions and is where traumatic memory "grooves" or soul wounds are processed and stored. It is also where the limbic system is located. This system causes us to have a fight-or-flight response when we perceive danger. When traumatic childhood memories are triggered, we often feel this as danger and have a fight-or-flight response, even though the danger is not in the present.

We humans are the only mammals that have a highly developed neocortex. Although other animals have a neocortex, particularly other primates, it is not as advanced in its functioning. Since other mammals do not have a sophisticated frontal lobe, they must depend more on their old brain or cerebellum for functioning. Unfortunately when it comes to traumatic memories, we humans often do the same thing. Why is this a problem?

Unlike the neocortex, the old brain formulates responses and behaviors by matching present patterns of sensory experience with past patterns. Simple and primitive, it makes broad distinctions related to safety and survival that are not always accurate. It is unable to make subtle distinctions according to circumstances, and its knee-jerk responses are typically blown out of proportion to current stimuli. These extreme survival responses become ingrained as they are recorded and stored in the old brain and create unhealthy habituated responses for us. This is why, for example, combat veterans relive trauma when they hear a car backfire or people who have a great deal of rejection from the past can overreact to even the slightest frown from a loved one (or anyone else!). To the old brain, all threats can be life-threatening. The more past trauma you have, the more you can overreact to real or perceived trauma in the present.[1]

Another key fact about the old brain is that it has no sense of time, which means a person can experience a traumatic soul wound at age five that can be triggered at age 35 and can feel the same intense emotion that he or she did as a child. The problem is that the individual is probably not in the same amount of risk or danger. The old brain is just overreacting.

We once had a client who was burned in a fire when he was four years old. As an adult, he still had the same fight-or-flight response when he smelled smoke. So you see, when your childhood wounds are triggered, you can overreact in much the same way you did as a child. Now, it's one thing to be burned in a fire, but what if your soul wounds are more emotional in nature? What if they were inflicted by those closest to you, like your mother or father? These wounds can then be triggered by those closest to you in your adult life—your spouse and children. This explains why there can be such volatility in families.

Frequently, people are angrier with their spouses (and children) than they were with their parents. This is because as children it was taboo to express anger toward their parents. But as adults they do not have as many sanctions on their emotions and they feel more freedom to let their toxic feelings out. Transgenerational theorist Murray Bowen called this phenomenon "putting your parent's face on your partner."[2]

Bill and Amy recognized that they did just that. Bill realized that his father wounded his soul with his verbal and physical abuse. He was not allowed to get angry with his father, but he would "put his father's face" on Amy and rage away, then fall into a sullen pit and withdraw.

Amy, too, saw that she had childhood soul wounds. Her father was never critical or abusive, like Bill's dad, but his quiet workaholic nature caused him not to give Amy the attention and approval she needed as a child. When Bill withdrew from her and the children, her old brain was triggered, and she put her father's face on Bill. She then reacted in much the same way she had done as a child. Only this time she gave it even more emotion. As a child she felt powerless, but as an adult she actually thought she could get someone to listen to her.

As Bill and Amy fully expressed their inordinate anger and emotion at each other and their children, they gave situations more emotion than they deserved. When this happens it can trigger physiological responses—the heart races, the chest gets tight, you might see red. This is because the old brain's autonomic nervous system is set off as well. This phenomenon is called *reactivity*. We define *reactivity* as giving a situation more emotion than it deserves because a childhood soul wound is being triggered.

Learning about the old brain and reactivity was very freeing for the Smiths. Bill actually said that at times he thought he was a crazy rageaholic like his father, whose behavior he abhorred. Many people, like Bill, feel like they are bad people or bad Christians because reactivity keeps them from practicing emotional self-control. It is hard to practice the fruit of the Spirit when your brain function is working so hard against you.

There were many times Tom and I could relate to couples like the Smiths. In our early marriage, we would trigger each other's soul wounds and become reactive to one another. After a fight I would wonder if I was mentally ill like my mother, or even demon possessed! Tom felt like a failure as a Christian leader because he let his anger overtake him. We tried fasting, praying, and Bible reading to stop these unhealthy patterns, all to no avail. It was such a relief for us to learn about the old brain and how it can torment us. It explained so much about those fights we had so many years ago. Recognizing that there was a biological reason for our emotional outbursts was a truth that began to set us free, and it helped us see that we were not deranged or evil! We saw that we were simply human and very wounded, which was the beginning of our soul-healing journey.

Once we became aware of our triggers and subsequent reactivity, we could attach it to our childhood soul wounds. This helped us to separate our current emotions from the hurt and pain of the past, stop our unhealthy reactivity, and give our present situation only the energy and emotion that it deserved. We could then ask the Lord to help us practice self-control instead of reactivity. This did wonders for healing our marital conflicts. In becoming more aware of our own and each other's soul wounds, we could pray for the healing that the Lord so graciously provided.

In order to develop lasting change in our marriage, we had to work to understand our reactivity on a much deeper emotional level. We began to understand the issues, actions, and attitudes that had created our soul wounds and learn about and accept the idea of reactivity. But we soon realized that this wounding process goes much deeper than just actions and learned responses. We discovered that there are also deeper messages from these soul wounds that "teach" us who we are and how we are to behave in relationships. The next chapter deals with those messages.

Chapter Four

The Message of Our Soul Wounds

*I*n our work we have learned that old brain reactivity is not the only thing detrimental about soul wounds. We have found that every soul wound creates a *message*. The problem with this message is that we internalize it and believe it is true about us. This is especially true if the wounds came from our parents because we had little choice but to believe them. As infants, our first impression of our parents is that they are all-powerful. They can bring dark and light into our limited universe simply by flipping a switch. They are our only source of food and shelter. Our infant screams are about our need for their sustenance. Parents, then, have a great deal of power over the psyches of their children, and this power can be misdirected or misused.

Not only do we internalize the messages of our soul wounds, but we generalize them as well, which means that we believe the messages are true in every context of our lives. So, we not only believe the messages of our wounds, but we believe that everyone believes them about us as well. Our parents' verbal and nonverbal messages become tattooed on our souls, and we spend a lifetime trying to prove that they are not true, all the while unconsciously (and often consciously) believing that they are.

The Message of Bill's Soul Wounds

Bill saw that the message of his wound was that he was not good enough. He said that he had believed that message all of his life, yet when he tried to recall specific instances from childhood, he drew a blank. It is typical for people not to be able to recall painful childhood memories. This is because the psyche has a way of blocking them out of our conscious minds. But they are still present in our unconscious, and the Lord can graciously bring them to our recollection if we ask. The Holy Spirit is a gentleman, and will not show us these memories to cause us more pain. He does this in order to heal us.

As we were helping Bill remember his childhood and the soul wounds that resulted, we took him to the prophet Isaiah once again. "I will give you the treasures of darkness, riches stored in secret places, so that you may know that I am the Lord, the God of Israel, who summons you by name" (Isaiah 45:3). The Lord knows us by name. He knows all of our repressed wounds, and desires to reveal them to us. He does this, not in order to blame our parents, cause us pain, or have us defer responsibility for our actions. He shows us these secret hiding places of childhood soul wounds to set us free.

As we prayed, Bill began to remember. He sat there sober and serious, leaning forward on the sofa. The look of pain enveloped him. There was no hint of the characteristic sarcasm in his voice. He looked at us with anguished eyes that were fearful but wanting to trust that we would understand.

"I was the middle of three boys," he began softly. "My oldest brother followed in my father's footsteps, and started using drugs as a teenager, a habit he still continues today. My younger brother is serving time in jail for armed robbery. I took a different path. When I was ten years old, I started going to mass with my grandmother, who lived next door. I even went to confirmation class as a teenager, but my parents didn't attend my confirmation ceremony. I never understood that. My brothers got more attention than me and I tried to be the good kid." Bill's voice broke as he shared and he tried hard not to cry.

"The church helped me stay on the straight and narrow. I worked my way through college and landed a great job as a banker, where I guess I did well, better than my brothers at least. But my father never acknowledged my success, and spent most of his time lamenting about the few things I didn't do. I tried for years to win my father's favor, but I just couldn't seem to crack his angry, critical veneer. Finally, I gave up trying." It was obvious that the message that scarred Bill's soul was *I'm not good enough.*

THE MESSAGE OF AMY'S SOUL WOUNDS

While the Isaiah passage was helpful for Amy, she recognized that her truths were not so hidden. Her father was a quiet, moody workaholic who spent little time with her and her older sister. Her sister was the family rebel. Amy watched as her sister got into trouble for skipping school, sassing her parents, and staying out all night with her shady friends. Amy was the good girl. She made good grades, excelled at sports and band, but never seemed to get her father's attention. Her futile attempts to get his approval caused her to believe this message: *I am not important; no matter what I do, I do not matter.* This eventually caused her to seek negative attention from boys when she grew older. Amy feared this would happen to Chloe if she didn't win Bill's approval.

We shared with the Smiths that the messages of our soul wounds cause responses or ways of adapting to help us deal with the pain. We call these responses *adaptations.*

ADAPTATIONS

An adaptation is how we respond to the messages of our soul wounds. They are the behaviors that we enact to cope with the hurt. Bill's adaptation was to try hard in the beginning to gain someone's favor or recognition, and then give up when he saw it was unsuccessful. Upon giving up, he would withdraw from people and situations. His sullen distance and aloofness were adaptations to deal with his lifelong wound of rejection.

Amy's adaptation was to overreact and be overly emotional, which was the opposite of Bill's pulling away and shutting down. Once again we see that opposites attract. Amy would try harder in situations, in order to feel that she was important or that she mattered. Her adaptation caused her to become over-involved at the kids' school, overcommitted at church, and too invasive and intrusive in Bill's life, often not respecting his privacy. As you can imagine, this caused a great deal of trouble for Bill and the children.

Bill's distance triggered Amy's message of not feeling important and she responded with her adaptation by becoming over-involved in his life. She did this by begging, pleading, and fixing, and then criticizing Bill for not responding. This criticism hit Bill's deepest wound, and his response (acting in his adaptation) was to distance and withdraw love and approval. This was the very thing that wounded Amy even more. So again she responded with her unhealthy adaptive behaviors, which triggered Bill's adaptations. They were in a crazy cycle of wounding each other in the same way they were wounded by their parents, and as a result they were overreacting to these wounds. This became the crux of their marital and family power struggle, which we will talk about later in this book. But for now, this couple had to focus on asking the Lord to heal their soul wounds. They needed a way to heal their hurts.

As we have done so many times before with hurting couples, we leaned toward them, asking the question that would change their lives. "Bill and Amy, do you know that God wants to heal you?" I asked gently. They both looked apprehensive yet hopeful, both wanting to believe this great truth amidst lifelong doubt. Many of us doubt that the Lord can heal our deep soul wounds. Perhaps it is because they have been with us for so long and are so deep-seated. Or maybe they have such a stranglehold on our lives that we secretly believe that they are too big even for the Lord to heal.

With as much compassion as my heart could muster, I began to share with this precious couple. "Jeremiah 30:17 in the King James Version says, 'I will restore health unto thee, and I will heal thee of thy wounds.' You have spent a lifetime blaming yourselves, feeling responsible, and experiencing the effects of these wounds. Unfortunately the wounding started with your parents, but it will end with the Lord's love and soul healing. You have spent too many years believing unhealthy messages and adapting in unhealthy ways. The Lord, our Redeemer, wants to redeem all of this for you. He wants you to know that what happened to you as children was not your fault." I repeated it again gently, "It was not your fault. Can you say this with me?" I asked, still slowly repeating this healing phrase, "It was not my fault." It took a few tries for them, but we could hear their faint murmurs as they struggled to say the words. These are words we all long to hear when we suffer from childhood wounds.

Soon Bill and Amy started to speak in unison. At first, their voices were a mere whisper, but eventually they became a confident roar. As they spoke, tears filled Amy's eyes—tears of joy that the once haunting messages were not true. Bill did everything he could not to cry. He did not want to look at the pain he had been repressing beneath his anger for so many years. But his tears finally betrayed him. They both then started to weep as the self-recrimination, self-blame, and negative self-talk that had tormented them for years began to disappear. Because Tom and I have experienced God's soul-healing love so many times, we knew the relief and joy they felt and we cried with them.

Paula Rinehart in her great book *Perfect Every Time* gives words to these soul tears when she says, "When we finally realize God's love for us, we are rent of our well-crafted defenses. And it is in this awkward nakedness, we begin to discover the substance of our soul [wounds and all]. It is through wading into this kind of brokenness—rather than running away—that we experience an increasing sense of wholeness and dependence on God. . . . God has always seen past our defenses and knows us as we are. It is His relentless pursuit of us that gives us the courage to come out of hiding."[1]

After a brief pause, Bill gave us another taste of his trademark sarcasm as he joked, "I swore I wouldn't let you guys make me cry. I guess that's what I get for swearing." The levity brought a natural pause to the deep work we were doing as we all had a good chuckle. Bill and Amy breathed a sigh of relief as the burden of their pasts began to lift from their souls. We then prayed with them to receive this gift of healing that the Lord had offered them. We asked them to pray daily for the healing of their own and each other's souls, and for the souls of their children.

THE WISDOM OF A SAGE

In order for Bill and Amy to truly believe that the messages of their wounds were not true, and their adaptations unnecessary, they had to look at them in the light of God's Word. Again we led them to the great scribe Isaiah. Isaiah 41:9–10 says, "I took you from the ends of the earth, from its farthest corners I called you. I said, 'You are my servant'; I have chosen you and have not rejected you. . . . do not be dismayed, for I am your God. I will strengthen you and help you; I will uphold you with my righteous right hand." God's Word dispels the messages of our wounds by saying that we are worthy, important, and lovable, and we're the apple of His eye. We instructed Bill and Amy to go to God's Word regularly to reinforce their daily healing and restoration.

More than once in our lives, this Isaiah passage has been a beacon of light for Tom and me as we struggled not to believe the messages of our soul wounds and act out our unhealthy adaptations to them. These words were also a balm for Bill and Amy. Allow them to be a beacon of healing for you as well.

THE SOLUTION

Below are several key questions that will help you recognize your soul wounds, where that wounding started, and what you can do about them. These questions will also help you determine the message of your soul wounds and how you adapted in unhealthy ways. Overcoming the messages of our soul wounds and our unhealthy adaptations requires the righteous right hand of the Lord to uphold us as we fight to dispel the lies we have believed most of our lives, so pray for wisdom if you have trouble remembering or answering. Answer these questions as honestly as you possibly can:

Step 1. What are your soul wounds and where did the wounding start?

All of us have suffered some kind of pain in childhood. There are no perfect parents or environments. Everyone has been wounded in some way. Ask yourself what those wounds might be and where they originated. Soul wounds can be active like abuse, or passive like neglect. Some are overt, such as incest, and some are more subtle, like feeling unloved or feeling like you're not good enough.

Perhaps you had great parents and a wonderful childhood but your wounds came from your environment. Were you teased or ridiculed by peers or neighbors? Did you move frequently and have a hard time forming attachments? Perhaps you felt different from everyone because of this. If you were an Irish Catholic and lived in an entirely Protestant neighborhood, you could have been wounded. If you were an artist in a family full of athletes, you could feel like you did not measure up. Your family may not have intended to wound you, but it happened nonetheless. Recognizing your soul wounds can help you understand a great deal about yourself and your relationships.

Step 2. What are the messages of your soul wounds?

As a result of your soul wounds, what messages do you believe about yourself? Do you feel unworthy, or that you are not important? Maybe you feel that you can never succeed. This message may have formed a theme for your life and this theme has tormented you for too long. Whatever the message is, write it down. Later you will learn more about what to do with this information.

Step 3. What are your adaptations?

How have you adapted to these soul wounds? What are the behaviors that you do as a result of the messages of your soul wounds? Do you distance and give up, or compulsively try to fix circumstances or situations? Perhaps you adapt by trying to do things on your own instead of trusting the Lord to help you. Whatever your adaptations are, it will help you to become aware of them as you write them down.

Step 4. Ask the Lord to heal your soul wounds.

As you recognize your soul wounds, their messages, and the unhealthy, often ungodly adaptations to them, you can ask one of the most important questions you will ask in your life: "Lord, will you heal me?" We know that God is fully capable of healing even the worst offenses to our souls and it is important to ask in faith, trusting in Him for our healing. Sometimes this healing comes all at once and in other situations it takes time. During that time we can rest assured that the Lord is teaching us valuable lessons as we wait for His healing touch.

Step 5. *What does the Word of God say about you?*

What does the Bible say about God's unconditional love for us? Use the words of Isaiah and other Bible passages to flood your mind with how much the Lord loves you. God's Word says that He has called you, chosen you, has not rejected you, and will help, strengthen, and uphold you with His hand. These are just a few of the passages that speak love to you. You may understand with your mind that God loves you, but do not experience it in your heart. Use God's Word to help you move understanding from your head to your heart. Read these passages regularly and allow them to heal your wounded soul. There are exercises later in the book to help you do this as well.

In reading this chapter, the Lord has probably shown you some soul wounds in your own life. Here is the healing homework for you and your spouse to share with each other and your children.

HEALING HOMEWORK

- ~ What situations in your marriage or family life can trigger your reactivity?
- ~ When you have reactivity, what do you do?
- ~ What are your soul wounds?
- ~ What can you do to change your harmful patterns and be healthier as a couple and as a family? Start by completing the steps above and sharing them with each other.

Chapter Five

The Sins of the Fathers: How We Pass Down Pain and Hurt

*B*ill and Amy had been coming to counseling faithfully for months. One March morning there was a springtime breeze in the air when they arrived at our office. Just as spring is pregnant with new life, they both seemed bursting with the newness of what the Lord was doing in their souls.

"We were talking on the drive over here about how much better things have been since we started coming to see you," Amy said, patting Bill's leg. "We still have struggles but now we feel like we can find a way out of them."

"We can find a way out of *most* of them," Bill corrected with a smile.

"We have news to share with you," Amy continued excitedly. "Bill let the kids and me get a puppy as an early Easter present!"

"I caved," Bill said. "They finally wore me down!"

"This is huge because the kids and I have wanted a puppy for years and Bill would not have it. He didn't want the responsibility and the mess, and he was sure the kids would not help with its care. About once a year the kids would beg him, and then get very disappointed when he refused. We were so surprised when he agreed, and so far the kids have been great."

"I can't believe I did it and I love the little guy. He's so cute!" Bill said with some excitement. We had rarely seen him express such enthusiasm, and were delighted to be a part of it. He and Amy found their traditional places on our sofa and by now they were sitting very close and the encouraging pats were going both ways.

"Bill hasn't been in his dungeon in weeks," Amy said. "Now that the weather is nice, we've taken the dog for walks almost every night. Bill has actually gotten pretty good at asking the kids questions, and he even made pancakes with them Saturday and did not yell at them once. This was amazing because Chloe dropped an egg and it splattered all over the floor," Amy explained. "Typically Bill would yell at her and the whole day would be ruined."

"I didn't yell," Bill proudly reported while patting Amy. "I feel like I'm changing and the best thing is that I feel the Lord with me more than I ever have before. One of the things I have realized in all of this soul healing is how bad my dad made me feel about myself and how it hurt me more than I knew. It has made me think about my own kids and how I may have wounded them. Normally, I would have yelled at Chloe, but now, most of the time, I try to think before I act."

"When parents begin to experience God's soul-healing love, it is typical for them to become aware of how they may be wounding their children," I told Bill and Amy, and then I praised them for their insight and the great changes they were making.

"All this time I thought I was a good dad," Bill reflected. "But now, I see that my distance and irritability wounded my kids the way my dad wounded me. I never wanted Chloe and Billy to feel the rejection that I felt." It seems that the Lord was teaching both Bill and Amy Healing Premise #3.

HEALING PREMISE #3:

*To the degree that you are wounded, you can wound
or be wounded by those closest to you.*

"The saying 'Children live what they learn' really applies here," I said. "As humans, we learn from our parents by their modeling. This means that wounded people can wound people. There's a saying about fishing in the Mississippi River: 'If you put your boat in the water and you don't paddle, you will automatically go south!' If you do not deal with your woundedness, your family relationships can go south as well."

THE GENERATIONAL TRANSMISSION OF DYSFUNCTION

When Tom and I were in school, we learned about what family therapists call the generational transmission of dysfunction, which is the tendency to pass down unhealthy patterns and ways of interacting to our children and our children's children, so that the painful cycle continues. This made so much sense to me because I remember hearing my mother and her siblings tell stories about their abusive father, my grandfather Esau.

Esau was the town drunk and spent most of his nights in the small country jail in their little town. He had a reputation for two things: drunkenness and abusing his wife and children. One incident the siblings shared made my blood curdle.

My grandfather did not allow his children to speak unless spoken to, especially at the dinner table. One evening my mother and her brothers and sisters were being typical children and got tickled at each other. The more my aunt tried to stop laughing, the more she laughed. Esau corrected her, but she could not stop. He saw this as a grave sign of disrespect and, in a drunken stupor, broke a glass plate and cut my aunt across the throat as punishment. My aunt sported a four-inch scar on her neck until the day she died. But that was nothing compared to the wounding of her soul! I believe that watching and experiencing this abuse contributed to my mother's mental illness.

Tom's father had a similar story of generational pain. Tom's grandfather was a well-off landowner in central California in the 1920s. He and his brother, Tom's great-uncle, got into a dispute over land ownership and his great-uncle murdered his grandfather. Yet another blood-curdling story! This left Tom's sweet Portuguese grandmother a penniless single mom with four children in the heart of the Depression. In desperation, she married a man who hated Tom's dad and his brother and sisters and put them to work as tenant farmers. This man exploited his stepchildren by gambling all of their earnings away while they sat outside the bar every Friday night. You can still hear the pain and anger in Tom's father's voice whenever he tells this story.

Both of our parents thought that we should be grateful that we were not treated as severely as they were. They, like Bill, thought they were great parents because they were not as bad as their parents. It is sad that my mother died without recognizing that she severely wounded her children and passed down the dysfunction to me and my sister and brothers.

I praise the Lord that when I was 12 years old, He led me to a little neighborhood church in my town. In church, I learned about Christ and His unconditional love for me. That love, along with the care of some sweet families in the church, helped me see how parents are supposed to treat their children. I watched the way my pastor and Sunday school teachers treated their families and vowed to be more like them.

One sultry summer day I sat on the old maple pew of that country church, and I heard the pastor preach about family. There was no breeze on that hot August Sunday and in those days there was no air conditioning, so all of us were fanning our bulletins in rhythm to the preacher's narrative. I listened intently as he quoted a scripture that leapt out at me: "For I, the Lord your God, am a jealous God, punishing the children for the sin of the fathers to the third and fourth generation of those who hate me" (Exodus 20:5b).

I sat perfectly still. The sweat beaded up on my forehead because I knew that God was speaking directly to me. As the pastor poured out his sermon about how sins can be passed down from generation to generation, stories of my abusive grandfather flashed through my mind. Echoes of my mother's abuse to me and my siblings barraged my psyche. I clenched that maple pew with my sweaty palms, and pleaded with the Lord silently, *Please Lord, please don't let this happen to me. I want to be a loving, caring, godly parent. I want this generational pattern to stop here!*

When I came out of my prayerful panic and once again became conscious of the pastor's discourse, I heard my fervent preacher finish the passage of Scripture: "but showing love to a thousand generations of those who love me and keep my commandments" (Exodus 20:6). There they were, the words the Lord wanted me to hear. I desperately needed to know that the abuse in my family would stop because I would choose to love and serve the Lord. He graciously allowed me to hear this wonderful truth.

Tom's generational healing came from his loving pastor who took him under his wing and mentored him after Tom's family disintegrated. When Tom was hurting over his father's indiscretions or his parents' divorce, he would call Reverend Tubbs. At a moment's notice this stately pastor would meet Tom for a cup of coffee and an encouraging chat. Sometimes they talked about Tom's pain and sometimes they simply talked about life. The wise reverend's mentoring was invaluable to Tom. He was a great husband and father and taught Tom how to change the future for his family. It was a joy for us both to have Reverend Tubbs do our premarital counseling and preside over our wedding ceremony some 32 years ago. We are so grateful to the Lord for having godly people cross our paths to show us the way out of our generational patterns of dysfunction.

IDOLATRY AND FAMILY PAIN

Tom and I have been studying Exodus chapter 20 for years. The awareness that God shows mercy to those who love Him and keep His commandments, and the help of some wonderful Christian people, have helped us break the generational chains in our families. We have claimed Exodus 20:6 for the healing of our children and our children's children: ". . . but showing love to a thousand generations of those who love me and keep my commandments."

The interesting thing about this scripture is that is located right in the heart of the Ten Commandments. This passage says that we should not have idols or worship anything but the Lord God Almighty. If you do, you, and the generations after you, will suffer. It is important to note that idols are not just golden calves or graven images; they can be anything that you put your time, energy, and faith in more than God. Work can be an idol, like it was for Amy's dad. Alcohol can be an idol, just as it was for my grandfather and Bill's father. These idols kept them from trusting God for their healing. In their wounded state, they wounded their children, and so the cycle continued.

Secular scholars in the field of family therapy thought that they had really discovered something amazing when they unearthed the concept of the generational transmission of dysfunction. Little did they know that God had already revealed it to us thousands of years ago in His Word!

Ask yourself what the idols are in your own life and family. Are they work, success, or wealth? Many an executive has sat in our office lamenting about losing his family as he climbed the corporate ladder, making success his idol. Perhaps your children are your idol. That can't be bad, you think; at least you love them as God desires. But you vicariously live your life through them, or worry so much about them that they become more important to you than the Lord. Idols consume our time and energy and leave little left to relate to Our Creator.

The worship of idols was rampant in Isaiah's day and God used Isaiah to warn His children about this destructive practice. We can learn more about this from hearing once again from this wise prophet.

THE WISDOM OF A SAGE

Isaiah lived in Judah, which is now southern Israel. Judah's righteous king Uzziah had passed away. In their grief, the people of the land turned toward idolatry. This grieved God's heart and He instructed Isaiah to warn the people about their unhealthy, ungodly practices. Because of their pain and selfishness, they did not listen. Isaiah 44:6, 9-11a says, "This is what the Lord says—Israel's King and Redeemer, the Lord Almighty: I am the first and I am the last; apart from me there is no God. . . . All who make idols are nothing, and the things they treasure are worthless. Those who would speak up for them are blind; they are ignorant, to their own shame. Who shapes a god and casts an idol, which can profit him nothing? He and his kind will be put to shame."

Isaiah is clear: Idolatry is futile. If you are struggling with an idol in your life, you are endangering yourself and your family and your children's children. Once you recognize your idols and begin to see how detrimental they are to your relationship with those closest to you and with the Lord, you can ask the Lord to help you renounce them. We will learn more about how to do this later, but first, let's look at the negative effects this idolatry may have already had on your family—especially your children.

What About the Kids

As people become aware of the damage done to them by the generations who came before, they frequently become concerned about how they may have wounded their children. By far, one of the most frequently asked questions by participants in our Soul Healers Weekend is "How can we stop passing the pain and dysfunction from our parents down to our children?" Tom and I lead them to a wonderful book that inspired us many years ago, James Dobson's classic *Parenting Isn't for Cowards*. This question was asked of Dr. Dobson by newly Christian parents who realized that they raised their children by the wrong principles before they became Christians. While the context is a little different, the answer still applies. Dr. Dobson said, "We don't always handle our children as unemotionally as we wish we had, and it's very common to look back a year or two later and see how wrong we were in the way we approached a problem. All of us experience these failures! That's why each of us should get alone with the Creator of parents and children and say, 'Lord, You know my inadequacies. You know my weaknesses . . . Make up for the things I did wrong. Satisfy the needs that I have not satisfied. Wrap Your great arms around my children, and draw them close to You.'"[1]

God loves us and He loves our children even more than we do. He is big enough to help us heal the wounds we have inflicted upon our children and turn our hurting family into a healing one. It is not that we stop disciplining our children. In fact, as we experience soul healing, we desire that our children follow the Healer's principles even more. The difference is that we lead by example, and correct them with love, not unhealthy anger. In order to stop the generational transmission of dysfunction, you need to focus on disciplining your children rather than punishing them.

Discipline Versus Punishment

Often when Tom and I deal with parents, we see that they try to shape their children's unhealthy behaviors by focusing too much on punishment. These parents spend most of their time spanking, grounding, or taking away privileges. By the time they come to counseling they have taken away virtually everything from their kids and still their misbehavior is not curtailed. Too much emphasis on punishment can be ineffective and harmful. The objective is to discipline behavior in order to shape it for the Lord, not to punish a child to "teach him or her a lesson." Discipline is instructive. Punishment is punitive. Too much punishment without loving instruction can provoke your children to wrath and cause them to rebel.

The goal of disciplining your children is to know them so well and love them so much that you find a way to share the ways of the Lord in a language they will understand. In doing this, you strive to teach them Christian principles so well that they will be second nature to them. They will consciously and unconsciously know God's ways, as well as His great soul-healing love, like the back of their hand. When they have a firsthand knowledge of both, for them *not* to follow godly principles would take an act of their will. In order for this to happen, you have to balance judgment and mercy when the situation calls for both. This is no easy task and needs to be done with God's supernatural help and guidance.

The context for such help and guidance is that you always focus on what is best for your children *in the dynamic* of your relationship with them. In other words, you let your discipline always be for the good of your relationship with them and their relationship with God. This will help you balance judgment and mercy because that is what the Lord has given to you as well. It will lead you to the characteristics we describe in the next chapter, the solution to stopping the unhealthy cycles of the past and fostering true healing in the present and future.

Chapter Six

The Solution: Understanding and Connection

*I*n the 27 years Tom and I have spent raising our daughters, there have been two key concepts that have helped us more than anything else. These concepts have helped us stop the cycle of abuse and dysfunction from our families of origin—to be healers of our children instead of wounders. These keys are *understanding* and *connection*.

UNDERSTANDING

When our children were one and three, we heard a great radio series on parenting by Chuck Swindoll. He shared Proverbs 22:6 which says, "Train up a child in the *way* he should go, and when he is old he will not depart from it" (NKJV) (emphasis mine). As parents, Tom and I had always thought that this scripture meant that we were to train up a child in the way we, as wise godly parents, thought he or she should go. Swindoll makes the point that in the Hebrew, the word *way* is *derek*, which actually means "bent" or "characteristics distinctive to" the person. So the real meaning of this verse is train up a child according to *his or her bent or distinctive characteristics*. In other words, get to know your children's unique characteristics. Discover their gifts and abilities, and encourage them to live their lives accordingly. Don't try to make an artist into an athlete. Don't force a tone-deaf child to be an opera star. In order to determine the bent in your children, you will have to spend time with them and listen to what they are saying—especially to what they are not saying. You have to get to know who each child really is.

Finding the bent in our daughters made all the difference in our raising them. Amanda, our oldest daughter, was the quintessential strong-willed child. In the first three years of her life we wore out the pages of James Dobson's great book *The Strong-Willed Child*. It remained on my nightstand long into her teen years because I frequently needed it for instant reference. We managed to channel much of Amanda's strong will and intelligence, and when she started school, she made great grades and won many academic and character awards.

Nicole, our younger daughter, had a completely different bent. Nikki was a free spirit who was driven to laugh, play, and enjoy people. She did not need a great deal of scolding when she made a mistake and would typically obey immediately. When she started school she was not as driven as her sister so she was not a straight-A student. However, Nicole had great people skills. She loved to talk, share, and connect with people. Unfortunately, this caused her to get lower marks in conduct. We had to find a way to affirm her bent and still discipline her behavior, all the while fighting the urge to compare the two girls. It was even hard for their teachers not to expect superior performance from Nicole. We began to see how wounded she was as they compared her to her sister. We heard things like "Nicole doesn't have the extraordinary penmanship that her sister has." "Nicole doesn't get as many gold stars in conduct as her sister did." It was not that these teachers were malicious or intending to harm our daughter; they simply were succumbing to their human nature to compare children.

Finally, it became obvious that we had to send her to a different school. This meant that we had to drive two car pools, attend two sets of school functions, and try to manage two different school calendars. But it was important in understanding and affirming their bents.

This made a world of difference for both girls. Nikki bloomed as she shed the shadow of her older sister, and their distance made them appreciate each other more. It is true, understanding who your child really is can help her determine who she is and what the Lord has for her life. In this way your children can be fully, authentically themselves. By the way, Nicole's bent toward talking, sharing, and connecting ended up working well for her as she chose marital and family therapy as a career. Amanda's academic bent has made her a great financial analyst. We were glad we got to know their gifts and abilities, which helped them find their places in this world.

CONNECTION

The second great key to being a soul-healing parent is *connection*. As we understand who our children really are, and accept and encourage them to be all that the Lord created them to be, we have to make a connection with them. Webster's 1991 edition has several definitions for *connection* and they all apply to healthy soul-healing parenting.

The first is *having influence or power over someone*. Parents have automatic power over their children by virtue of their position, and this should not be misused. In our counseling practice we have seen too many parents fail to make a connection with their children because they misuse their parental authority and thus provoke their children to wrath, as Ephesians 6:4 says.

Connection also means *a channel of communication*. Parents who desire to heal the souls of their children communicate openly with them. They also allow their children to be open with them. This means that you have to fight the urge to overreact when 16-year-old Emily tells you that her friend Ali is taking birth control pills. You want her to confide in you, and overreaction can quell this quickly. There is also a delicate balance between being too intrusive into your child's life, and being uninterested or preoccupied with your own issues. Single parents have an extra burden in this area, as they often have to play the roles of both mother and father, with all of the extra responsibilities that go with this.

Webster's also tells us that *connection* means *a circle of friends*. Being in your child's circle of friends is an awesome honor. You want to be the one they confide in, but you have to find a balance between being a friend and maintaining your authority as a parent. You do this by expressing openness, love, and a healthy balance between judgment and acceptance.

Finally, our definition of *connection* means *connecting to the souls of your children as they connect to yours*. Know them—their gifts, abilities, goals, passions, and dreams. Listen when they tell you about their sorrows and heartbreaks. Be there when they win, and especially when they lose. Hear them when they tell you that you are too controlling or too distant. Listen when they say that you have to trust the way you raised them and let them grow up. Love their souls, connect to their souls, and heal their souls. The Lord will reward you greatly for your efforts.

THE REST OF THE STORY

Tom and I finished this chapter of the book on Memorial Day weekend. We took a much-needed break and went to the grocery store around the corner to get food and supplies for our annual family cookout. Our family loves this holiday because Tom grills his famous barbecued hamburgers, and I make my renowned orange Jell-O salad. Family celebrations are particularly important for me because when I was growing up, we never had any. In my home there were no birthdays, no Christmases, no Easters, much less minor holidays like Memorial Day. Tom remembers a few celebrations before he was 13, when everything in his family went dark. So, you can see why family get-togethers are very special to us.

As we were shopping, a couple approached us. "Bev and Tom, do you remember us?" the wife asked. "Of course," I replied "How are your daughters?" About a decade before, they had come to our clinic for family therapy. Their oldest daughter, Emmy, had rebelled, dropped out of college, and was hanging out with some unsavory folks. Their younger daughter got caught in the crossfire, and felt neglected and lost because her parents spent so much time and energy on her older sister. "You were so right," the mom shared, "when you taught us how to connect to Emmy's soul. After seven years, and a few stops and starts, she finally finished college, with pink hair no less! We were so proud of her." They proceeded to tell us more about their younger daughter who was in graduate school studying architecture.

We had finished our conversation and were strolling down the produce aisle when we saw another familiar face. By now, you are probably thinking that Charlotte is a small town, but it isn't. "Bev and Tom, how are you?" an older woman with an inviting smile asked. "Remember our son Brent, and how worried I was that we would pass down the same pain to him that we went through with our own parents? You helped us through such a rough time then. Do you recall how he and my husband did not see eye-to-eye on anything?" she asked excitedly, unable to wait for an answer. "Well, you would not believe it. Brent is now working with his dad! He's in the sales department of my husband's company. You said that understanding and connection would eventually heal our family, and it did."

"I think your prayers and persistence helped as well," I added. When we finished our conversation, we left the grocery store totally filled up with God's goodness, just as we had so many times before when the Lord would bless us with these divine encounters. But all of this paled in comparison to the phone calls we received on our short trip home from the store. "Mom, we're in Charlotte!" our older daughter said excitedly, as she and her new husband were traveling home from a visit to his parents'. "We can't wait to see you. Are you ready for our cookout?" This was music to our ears as parents. The call was interrupted. I struggled to work the call-waiting feature on my new cell phone. It was our younger daughter calling. "Mom, I'm in Virginia and should be home by five o'clock," she said. She was on her way home from Denver Seminary where she was studying Christian counseling.

"I can't wait to see y'all. I have missed you so badly. I've learned so much and you are the first people I wanted to share it with. After studying counseling, I want you to know that you and Dad are my inspiration. I want to be just like you!" This moved me emotionally in a profound way. You see, I never wanted to be like my mother. In fact, I strove to be her opposite. Tom did the same thing. When he was a boy, Tom idolized his father and wanted to be just like him. But after his family fell apart he never desired to emulate his dad again. This is why it meant so much to us that our children looked up to us. We both had a good grateful cry that afternoon as we put the groceries away.

We never set out to inspire our children to be like us. This task was much too daunting. We just desired not to make our parents' mistakes. We simply strove to not pass down the sins of our parents to them. It was important to us that our children knew that they were loved for who they were, for who God made them to be. Attempting to be soul-healing parents, we laughed with them and cried with them (when the coveted class presidency went to someone else). We lived with them and died with them (when the object of their crush started dating their best friend). We hurt with them and prayed with them (when they wanted more of our Lord, and sometimes when they didn't). We knew with them, and grew with them (when we had to hold on, and when we had to let go). We fought with them and loved with them (when we learned how to break a will without breaking a spirit). We feared with them and trusted with them (when we watched them become grown-ups, peers, and friends).

We did all of this so that they could be the healthy, happy, fulfilled, unique women God created them to be. The sleepless nights, worry, anger, conflict, heartache, empathy, pain, joy, happiness, and fulfillment were all worth it. We could not have done any of this without the supernatural help of the Holy Spirit, and we thank the Lord for His everlasting love that heals us all, over and over again

THE SMITH FAMILY

Like Tom and me, the Smiths didn't want to be like their parents either. After learning about idolatry, understanding, and connection, Bill and Amy began to recognize that they were in danger of repeating the unhealthy patterns they learned in their families of origin. They repented of the things they had done to their children and the things they had not done. Most importantly, both of them started to see that they had idols in their lives. Amy confessed that church work had been hers. Like many people, she dove into church work because it garnered praise from people, which helped her ailing self-esteem and took her mind off of her family woes.

Bill admitted that work and solitude were his idols for the same reasons. We praised their great insight. They also realized that their idols kept them from understanding and connecting to their children. Both of them prayed for forgiveness for that as well. Then they went home and sat their children down and told them how much they loved them. They told Chloe and Billy about their commitment to change the way they did some things in their family and apologized for their shortcomings as parents. Billy and Chloe listened intently to their parents' heartfelt confession and commitment to change. Bill and Amy then affirmed their children's individual bents and praised them for their gifts and abilities. Both Chloe and Billy beamed, which brought tears to Amy and Bill's eyes as they felt God's soul-healing presence envelop them.

13

What about you? After reading this chapter, has the Lord made you aware of how the sins of the fathers of generations before you may have caused harm to you and your family? It may be great news to you that the Lord wants to heal these patterns. Perhaps you have recognized idols in your life and are impressed that the Lord desires to take them away. You may have seen that you yearn for a deeper understanding and connection with your children and would like to affirm their particular bents more. Here are some questions and suggestions that may help you and your family.

HEALING HOMEWORK

~ Pray and ask the Lord to show you the generational patterns that you want to change in your family. Write them down, and pray a prayer of healing for all of you.
~ Write down the behaviors that you desire to change because of your generational healing.
~ List any idols in your life that you desire to confess. Write a prayer of repentance and forgiveness and pray it regularly.
~ Record the particular bents in each of your children and ask your children to list what they perceive as being their own bents.
~ On a regular basis, have a special dinner for each family member, where you pay tribute to him or her according to his or her bent (Mom and Dad too). Praise them for these distinctive behaviors, skills, and abilities and share what you like most about them. It will do wonders to create understanding and connection, and your family will love it!

Chapter Seven

The Nature of the Beast:
The Family Power Struggle

The cold Chicago wind seemed to blow through me, cutting me like a knife as I walked to my class at Northern Illinois University, where I attended graduate school. Tom and I had been married only six months when he moved me from the warm balmy climate of Los Angeles. I loved L.A. with its beaches, palm trees, and constant summer breeze. But as the dutiful wife, I traded it all to follow Tom to the dreaded frigidity of Illinois, where he had taken a job at a college.

I hated the cold weather. It snowed infrequently in the South where I grew up, and when it did, it was a glorious occasion. Schools were closed and work was cancelled. It was a time for snowmen, sleds, and eating snow cream. Illinois was a different story. When it snowed there, they didn't close schools, offices, or churches. They marched on and trudged through the frozen stuff.

Don't get me wrong, the first snowfall was beautiful with its stunning white powder covering the landscape. Pine trees looked like crystal angels. Elms and maples wore icy shawls outlining their silhouettes. It was magical! But then it stayed, and stayed—and stayed. Colder and colder it grew until I thought I'd never see green grass again. In fact, I didn't see grass from October until May! That was tough for this southern girl.

I began to resent Tom for taking me away from what I considered the best climate on earth. But we had been married less than a year and I didn't want to make waves. Because my parents fought so much and finally divorced, I falsely concluded that fighting led to divorce. I vowed never to fight in my marriage, which I now know is a big mistake. I avoided conflict at all costs, and as a result shoved my resentments down deep in my soul. I mistakenly thought that I was practicing a gentle, quiet spirit, like the Word talks about in 1 Peter 3:4. What I now know from research is that stonewalling is the highest predictor of divorce in marriages.[1]

What did I know then? I was 22 years old and fresh out of a really dysfunctional family that gave me no role models to follow in building a healthy marriage. Tom's situation was not much better. His parents' form of resolution was also dissolution. So as children of divorce, we didn't have much experience dealing with marital conflict and felt like fish out of water. Not only that, when we were first married we were daunted by the knowledge that children of divorce are at high risk for divorce themselves.

As I walked to my graduate class that day some 30 years ago, the wet snow pelted my face. *Why has he brought me here to this desolate frozen wilderness?* I thought, as the icy cold and resentment coursed through my veins. *I was headed for graduate school at USC until I met him. It's so unfair that I'm giving up my dreams for him.*

The trigger for my internal rant was a disagreement we'd had that morning about money. Tom wanted to buy a new stereo because ours was ancient. I said that we didn't have enough money. Because I grew up poor, I was a compulsive saver. Tom used to say that I could pinch a penny until Lincoln's eyes popped out! Now I can laugh about this, but then it devastated me. After every unresolved conflict, we hurt each other a little more. Looking back, we handled our unresolved conflicts poorly by distancing from each other and diving into our own interests. Tom was very busy in his new job as a college administrator and I poured myself into my classes in marital and family therapy.

We had been married less than a year and I thought that he had betrayed me. The man who had courted me and talked to me for hours on end now came home from work late and planted himself in front of the television, which, I was sure, he loved more than me. What had happened to our wonderful courtship? I was positive he had tricked me into marrying him by showing me only his good side—and he was convinced that I had changed as well. After every disagreement, we were more and more miserable.

I absolutely hated conflict, so situations like these took their toll on me, and my resentment mounted. The distance that occurred when we disagreed created such anxiety and pain for me that I could hardly stand it. Tom hated it too, but his adaptation to childhood wounds was to distance, so he felt safer. I went there by default, and when I did, I felt lonely, hopeless, and despairing. When we would undergo these early marital difficulties, I needed someone to talk to. I craved a mother's compassionate ear and voice of wisdom. It was during that time that I discovered more healing words from the prophet Isaiah.

THE WISDOM OF A SAGE

Thumbing through my Bible as a new Christian, I stumbled upon Isaiah 66:13, which says, "As a mother comforts her child, so will I comfort you." I repeatedly read this passage for solace. I eventually started to see that during all of the years that my mother was missing in action, the Holy Spirit had been a mother to me. The term *Holy Spirit* means *paraclete*, or one who walks beside you. Healthy mothers walk beside you. Godly mothers nurture your soul as best they can as mere mortals. But my mother was incapable of nurturance, so I turned to the Holy Spirit who led me to the words of Isaiah when again and again I needed the brush of the gentle, soothing wind that can only come from Glory.

Rather than nourishing my ailing spirit, my mother wounded my soul often by withdrawing her love as a form of punishment. I never knew when she would explode and beat me for such horrific offenses as using too much toilet paper or spilling my drink on the floor! This physical abuse was difficult, but somehow her emotional abuse seemed more insidious. Once she did not speak to me for two weeks for not getting the clothes off the line immediately after she asked me to. Her icy coldness crushed me. Tom's distance triggered these soul wounds and my reactive response was to panic and push for resolution or closeness.

My adaptation wounded Tom, and here's why. Because of his father's affairs, Tom's mom got very close to him, too close, in fact. He became her confidant and "surrogate husband." She told him all about their marital fights and his father's indiscretions. Looking back, he could see that she needed some support, but her son was not the one for that job. Many mothers make this mistake. They are hurt by their husbands, and need comfort and approval so they share too much with their children. This enmeshment from Tom's mom wounded him and he would become reactive if he was pushed too hard or too soon toward closeness. Besides, he would tell me, he's Portuguese, and they are hot tempered when angered and need a while to cool down after a conflict.

We were in a terrible dilemma. I needed closeness to heal my soul wounds and he needed space to heal his. My attempts to get him to be close re-wounded him the way his mother had done, and his attempts to establish some distance wounded me the same way I was wounded as a child. We could not understand each other, connect to each other, or find a way out of our painful situation. It was horrible for both of us and we didn't know where to go or what to do. We were in what we now call "marital purgatory." You may have been there too. You can't hear each other or see eye-to-eye on anything, and the distance and pain are palpable to all. It is truly a power struggle!

I arrived at my graduate class that day so frozen that I didn't remove my hat, coat, or gloves. As you can imagine, the natives thought I was weird. Cold to me was 40 degrees. Cold to them was 40 below zero.

It just so happened that day that the topic of class was dealing with marital conflict—a godly coincidence if ever there was one.

"Money, sex, roles, in-laws, childrearing, and jealousy over time spent outside the marriage are the top issues that couples fight about and they can subsequently can lead to divorce," Professor Mark shared while stroking his Freud-like beard.

Well, that just about covers all the issues that Tom and I have been dealing with the past year, I thought. The next statement he made was like salve to a sore. "Conflicts in marriage are inevitable and normal," he continued. I could feel my body beginning to thaw.

"The absence of conflict is not the sign of a good marriage. You can't take two different people who were raised in two different environments, put them together and expect there to be no conflict. It just won't happen. Each person wants power and they struggle to get it. Power struggles are unavoidable." Off came the hat and gloves as I feverishly wrote down almost every word he said.

"Healthy couples fight; they just learn how to resolve their conflict in a way that is mutually satisfying to both." I threw off my coat and was in a note-taking frenzy. I don't think that I have ever had such an extreme case of writer's cramp.

Later, as I drove the 30-mile trek home from class, I realized that Tom and I were in the throes of a power struggle. As I sped past the

Illinois cornfields covered with white and gray snow mounds, I longed for both winter and the power struggle to be over.

Children of divorce often have a fear of doom in their marriages.[2] Learning that power struggles were normal somewhat quelled my internal fear that Tom and I were doomed. It also provided the motivation for me not to give up and to find a way out. Now, some 30 years later, we have a clear definition of a power struggle and a clear way out.

By the way, we did move from the frozen tundra of Illinois to the gorgeous green grass of North Carolina and that did wonders for us. After three decades in this warm climate, I think I've finally thawed out!

DEFINITION OF A POWER STRUGGLE

We define a power struggle as a relationship in which there is an underlying tension that is always there. It is characterized by fear that results in a breakdown in communication, which leads to assumptions. And in a power struggle, you always assume the worst, and project it onto your partner or family member.

When Tom and I would get into a power struggle, we had a difficult time communicating, which led us to indeed assume the worst about each other and our relationship. I assumed that he had tricked me into marrying him by showing me his loving, nurturing side, only to betray me by being distant and over-focused on work. He thought that I had scammed him by showing him my generous side, only to become stingy and penny-pinching after we got married. Now, more than three decades later, thousands of couples have entered our office with the same feelings of fear and betrayal. And over those years, we have discovered something that can help them. We have found that there is actually a neurobiological reason for these painful feelings of betrayal. Neurobiology strikes again!

Neurobiology and Betrayal

Remember the "love cocktail" we talked about in chapter 1? Couples feel a strong sense of euphoria when they fall in love, or as we like to say, trip into infatuation. These tricky brain chemicals cause us to see our loved one in the most positive light. We view him or her as almost messianic. But these sly substances were not made to last. Like any chemical, the body eventually builds up a tolerance to them and it takes more and more of them to get the giddy feeling of "being in love."

Researchers say that it takes about four years for the love cocktail to completely fade.[3] When the chemicals fade, our partner becomes a mere mortal again. Unfortunately, couples don't know this, so they feel terribly disillusioned when their partner is no longer a loving moth around their flame. Instead of making this realization, and saying that their mate has simply resumed human rather than iconic status, most couples feel tricked. Some, like Tom and me, who were hurt a great deal by the ones we loved, feel deceived and betrayed. We saw each other move from messianic status to Satan incarnate!

Learning about fizzling brain chemicals helped Tom and me see that we were not as wonderful as we once believed, but we were not as horrible as we now thought either. This knowledge enabled us to stop assuming the worst about each other when we were in conflict, and see that we indeed did not trick or betray one another. We could then see a clear path to resolve the power struggle.

Similarly, when Bill and Amy Smith first came into our office, they, too, were enmeshed in a power struggle. Both of them felt betrayed and assumed the worst about each other, much like Tom and I had done so many years before.

Amy assumed that Bill didn't care for her and the children because he would not spend much time with them. Bill assumed that Amy was critical and hard to please. The truth was that neither assumption was accurate, but they were the only ones that couldn't see this. Our mini neurobiology lesson helped them, just as it did us.

As time went on and their soul wounds began to heal, they noticed that their conflicts lessened but they still needed to learn some good conflict resolution skills. Because of this, they both knew exactly what we were talking about when we defined the power struggle for them. It also helped them to realize that power struggles are normal. This became healing premise #4:

HEALING PREMISE #4:
Power struggles are inevitable and you can resolve them.

We shared with the Smiths that studies show that conflict is unavoidable and all couples have at least three issues that they fight about. If they split and find another partner, they simply trade issues. In first marriages, the main cause for conflict and divorce is reported to be money. In second marriages, childrearing takes the number-one conflict spot.[4] We have found this to be true in our practice as well.

BILL AND AMY'S POWER STRUGGLE

One of Bill and Amy's hot topics was childrearing. While they had greatly improved, Bill said that he still felt that Amy was too soft on the children at times, letting them get away with too much without discipline. Amy said that Bill could be too hard because he couldn't stand unruly children.

"Amy can baby them too much," Bill reported.

"I don't baby them," Amy broke in. "I just feel that I have to protect them from Bill when he gets grouchy or harsh."

It seemed that the softer Amy became, the more Bill felt that he had to be hard. And the harder Bill became, the more Amy felt she needed to be soft. The softer she was, the harder he became, and so the crazy cycle went. Sadly, they were working against each other, both wanting the same thing—well-behaved, obedient children.

We learned in chapter 1 that couples marry their opposites, and childrearing is just one more area where this polarity can play out. These couples will be healthier if they move toward the middle of the behavioral and attitudinal continuum. In fact, moving toward the middle can help them become the Divine Us that the Lord desires for them to be. Remember, this Divine Us is a balance between the two attitudinal and behavioral extremes, and it makes for healthy interaction. Developing God's oneness also helps couples become balanced and grow to become everything that the Lord wants them to be.

In order for Amy and Bill to move toward their Divine Us, they had to feel safe with each other. For Amy to get tougher on the children, she had to feel safe and assured that Bill would not be too hard. For Bill to get softer, he needed to feel sure that Amy would be harder. They both had to simultaneously move toward the middle to bring about healthy change in the family, but this is not easy to do. When you do this, it can be very scary because you may wonder if your spouse will move with you. Because of this you both have to move at the same time.

As we shared this information with Bill and Amy, Tom suggested that they just change one aspect of their unhealthy cycle. "Bill, how about you taking the lead as the man, and stretching to soften up with the kids?" he asked.

"Are you kidding?" he said fearfully. "If I soften up, then we will both baby the kids. They will be horrible to deal with."

"This is a common misconception with parenting," Tom explained. "If one mate joins the other, they fear that the system will be imbalanced in an unhealthy way. It may appear so at first, but what family therapists have seen for years is that if one mate moves toward the middle, it encourages the other to do the same."

"Bill, if you soften a little, I predict that Amy will feel more freedom to be harder on the children," I encouraged.

They both were hesitant, reporting that they had tried this before, which made them reluctant to try again. After some coaching on our part, however, they realized that their only way out was to move toward the middle and once again find that Divine Us that the Lord called them to be. This was only part of the solution to the power struggle for Bill and Amy. Another important part was their realization that what they were fighting about was not really what they were fighting about. Typically when family members fight, there is usually an underlying issue. This issue can often be connected to their soul wounds.

SOUL WOUNDS AND THE POWER STRUGGLE

Bill and Amy thought that their power struggle was about childrearing, but that was only partially true. The deeper issue was that they were triggering each other's soul wounds. When Amy criticized Bill's parenting, she learned that she triggered his soul wound from his father's criticism and lack of approval. Bill then became reactive and gave the situation more emotion that it deserved, thus being harder on the kids than was necessary. When Bill was too hard on the kids Amy relived her childhood soul wound with her dad. The message of her wounds—*You don't matter*—rang in her ears and she became reactive and overprotective of the children. Amy's criticism and lack of respect wounded Bill, and Bill's anger and harshness with the children wounded Amy.

In most families, the parents' power struggle often infects the children. Not surprisingly, one of the biggest problems with the Smith children was their constant fighting with each other. Chloe would boss Billy around and sometimes hit him for taking the DVD remote or not watching what she wanted on the television. Billy would yell at Chloe and call her names like "ugly moron" and "idiot." He too would resort to hitting. Their fights were often a mirror of Mom and Dad's struggles, as Billy would yell and scream and Chloe would criticize and control. Neither would resolve their differences, and their parents' attempts to discipline them would be futile. Not only that, the continual fighting injured their souls, and so the cycle was perpetuated.

When parents do not agree or form a strong united front in their discipline, children know that they can manipulate to get what they want. Because their mom was soft, the Smith kids would play on her sympathy when their dad was heavy-handed. In this way, they never had to change their unhealthy behavior, so the Smith family power struggle continued, much to their disappointment.

Like Tom and I did, the Smiths had to learn to accept the reality of their power struggle and how it affected their children. They also saw that what they were fighting about was actually rooted in their own woundedness, causing them to rewound each other and perpetuate the cycle. We discovered several specific concepts to help them with their healing and would like to share them with you in the next chapter in the hope that they will be equally helpful to your family.

Chapter Eight

Disarming the Family Power Struggle

I n the Soul-Healing Love Model we have found several keys that will help families stop reacting when their soul wounds are triggered, and help them avoid hitting these soul wounds as much as possible. These keys will help families resolve their power struggles. They are *Mindfulness, Intentionality, Sacrifice,* and *Communication.*

MINDFULNESS

Mindfulness is a state of being aware and attentive to your own soul wounds, as well as the soul wounds of the members of your family. When family members trigger your soul wounds—and you can be sure that those closest to you can trigger you more than anyone else—you must choose to self-soothe and ask the Lord to soothe your pain rather than becoming reactive. Mindfulness enables you to do this. It also helps you to be compassionate, empathic, and careful when relating to other family members, so as not to trigger soul wounds within them. Mindfully controlling your tongue when hurt by those close to you can help you resolve family power struggles. James 1:26 says, "Anyone who says he is a Christian but doesn't control his sharp tongue is just fooling himself, and his religion isn't worth much" (TLB). Mindfulness helps family members speak words of edification, not pain, thus resolving the power struggle.

INTENTIONALITY

Intentionality is defined as the ability to act in a healing way no matter how you feel. In other words, put your feelings aside for the sake of health. We did not say to deny your feelings. Denial is pretending that the situation is not difficult or painful. Intentionality says it is difficult and painful, but you choose to act in a constructive rather than destructive way for the sake of having healthy family relationships.

Being intentional got its start in the treatment of alcoholics. Even though alcoholics might be dying for a drink, they were told to resist the urge and act as if they did not desire it. In time, they learned that they indeed did not want the drink. They realized that if we act a certain way, then the desired feelings will follow. Intentionality is allowing your behavior to usher in your emotions, not the other way around.

Romans 12:2 instructs, "Do not conform any longer to the pattern of this world, but be transformed by the renewing of your mind." Intentionality is renewing your mind with healing thoughts when your soul wounds are triggered. It also helps you see your family members in a more positive light. Philippians 4:8 tells us to think on only those things that are pure, lovely, good, and holy. Being intentional can help you do this.

SACRIFICE

Sacrifice is defined as the surrender or giving up of something valued for the sake of something having a higher value. In families, you give up your right to be reactive, or retaliate when triggered, for the higher claim of healthy, godly interaction.

Unfortunately, words like sacrifice and surrender are not used much in our culture today. Narcissism has permeated our society. Magazines like *Self, Me,* and *All About You* cover newsstands. Because of our self-focus as a nation, sacrifice is not a popular concept. It is hard for all of us to give up what we want. We desperately need supernatural help. We must call on the soul-healing power of the Holy Spirit to do this.

EXPLAINING THESE CONCEPTS TO CHILDREN

It can be challenging to explain deep concepts such as mindfulness, intentionality, and sacrifice to children. We encourage you to use words and illustrations on a level that they can understand. With children, mindfulness can become "paying attention," intentionality becomes "self-control and not getting even," and sacrifice becomes "giving instead of taking" and "sharing instead of hoarding." Tom and I have noticed that these concepts can resonate with even small children, and teaching them can grow your child's Christian character.

OUR POWER STRUGGLE

By now, you may be wondering just how Tom and I healed our power struggle back in the frozen Illinois days. Part of why I was so devastated the first year of our marriage was because no matter how hard we tried not to, we continued to wound each other. I read books on marriage by great Christian leaders in which love and respect were constant themes. Sadly, we just could not seem to comply. In order to heal my abandonment wound, I needed the closeness that Tom felt he could not give. In order to heal his enmeshment wound, Tom needed space, which I could not provide. To repair our relationship, we both had to learn mindfulness and intentionality so we could respond to each other in a healing way. We then had to sacrifice our own needs to meet each other's. We had to do this in spite of not getting our own needs met. We had to give unconditionally, whether we received or not. The only way we could stretch to give to one another out of our need was with the Lord's help. In fact, our motivation became God's sacrificial, unconditional love that enabled Him to sacrifice His only Son for us as lost sinners.

As I stretched to heal Tom's enmeshment wound, I stopped pushing so hard for closeness. The amazing thing is that Tom actually moved toward me more because he felt less pressure and more freedom to connect with me. Likewise, as Tom moved toward me to heal my abandonment wound, I no longer felt compelled to pursue him to heal my soul wounds, so I could distance without fear and spend more time alone or with others. This was a blessing to him. So you see that mindfulness, intentionality, and sacrifice, inspired by the Lord, helped us to stretch to heal each other and move ourselves out of marital purgatory and the dreaded power struggle.

COMMUNICATION

As families become intentional and sacrificial, they can more easily learn how to communicate. They are more able to hear what is going on inside each other, and what their deeper issues really are. Tom and I have developed a tool we use in the Soul-Healing Love Model that is designed to help families determine the deeper emotions underneath their anger and communicate with each other about them. This tool is called the GIFT Exercise.

THE GIFT EXERCISE

For years, psychologists have postulated that anger is not a primary emotion. Anger is actually a secondary feeling or response to a more primary emotion. If you are feeling angry, there are typically four deeper primary emotions underneath it. These are: Guilt, Inferiority, Fear, and Trauma (or hurt and pain).

When family members get angry, they typically either hurl or hide their anger. Hurlers externalize their anger. They yell, scream, and blame. Hiders internalize their anger by stonewalling, being icy, and rejecting. Both patterns can be destructive. We have found that if you can share the deeper emotions beneath your anger, you have a better chance of not hurling or hiding. Because you are thinking more rationally you also have a better likelihood of being understood and thus resolving conflict.

In order for you to remember the deeper emotions, we developed an acronym to help you. The Lord gave us the word GIFT. Each letter stands for one of the primary emotions rooted in anger:

Guilt

Inferiority

Fear

Trauma (hurt and pain)

This acronym can help family members discover their root emotions, and this can actually be a gift to them.

Think about it for a moment: What causes you to feel angry? If someone accuses you of missing church too much, you may get angry and defensive, but what you may be really feeling is guilt. When someone cuts you off in traffic, you may feel fear or inferiority. *This guy is going to kill us,* or *Who does that guy think he is?* you think to yourself as you feel fearful or put down (inferiority). Identifying these deeper emotions helps families deal with what is really going on within their souls.

We taught the Smith family the key concepts of mindfulness, intentionality, and sacrifice. Of course, we had to explain them on the children's level and instructed Bill and Amy to reinforce our lesson. We then shared with the Smiths how to do the GIFT exercise and gave each family member a chart listing the deeper emotions underneath anger. Chloe and Billy's homework assignment was to draw pictures to illustrate each emotion. They were free to use their crayons and allow colors to express emotion as well. If they needed to, they could ask their parents for help. In anticipation of doing artwork, they gladly agreed to the task. We invited the whole family back to try the GIFT exercise in the following meeting.

A week later the entire Smith family returned. As they entered the waiting room, Chloe and Billy wasted no time in rummaging through their backpacks to retrieve their drawings. Billy fished through his yellow bag and proudly sported a beautiful drawing of brightly colored stick figures.

"You did a great job on your homework," I commented. His big blue eyes brightened as we all walked toward the inner office. Not to be outdone, Chloe pulled her masterpiece out of her bright pink bag as the family took their usual places on our sofa. Amy put the book bags on the floor as Chloe and Billy competed to share their drawings.

"For fear, I drew a black bear," Billy blurted out. "I'm afraid of black bears. We saw one on our vacation in the Smoky Mountains last summer," he explained.

"I drew a snake," Chloe interrupted. "I hate snakes."

"I do too!" I added. "Let's see what you drew for guilt."

"We both drew a yellow sad face for guilt," Billy offered, as he pointed to his picture. "This is when we don't do our chores and Mom gets disappointed, so we feel bad."

Chloe broke in, "Mom helped us with inferiority. She said it means feeling put down." Amy smiled as she listened in. "This is a drawing of the kids at school teasing me and I'm sad because I feel put down," Chloe continued. "That's inferiority, right?"

"It is sad when friends are cruel, isn't it," I responded.

"I drew a picture of Chloe bossing me around and I feel put down. This is me getting mad," Billy said, as he pointed to a very unhappy blue stick figure with a red-faced girl hovering over him.

"You made my head too big," Chloe protested as we all, even Chloe, had a good laugh. Lastly, Billy pointed to a giant head that was crying. "This is for hurt. This is when someone hurts my feelings."

"You children seem to have a really good idea of what these feelings are all about," I said as they beamed with pride. We then praised Bill and Amy for their assistance in helping their children do this assignment.

"I think they helped me as much as I helped them," Bill said. "They know more about feelings and emotions than I do. As you know, my family did not allow feelings to come out, so this exercise really helped me."

"Maybe Dad can draw a picture for us next time," I teased, and we all laughed again.

THE SMITHS' GIFT EXERCISE

We then encouraged the Smith family to try the GIFT exercise, letting them know that we would be there to coach them. We went over the rules so that everyone was clear.

1. Don't accuse, blame, or shame. Say, "When you do this . . . I feel this . . ."
2. No interruptions. Let each person share his or her heart.
3. Be mindful and intentional as you think about what you and other family members are sharing. Fight the urge to react in unhealthy anger or get even.
4. Talk about what you will change as a result of doing this exercise.

We placed the chart in front of them for reference and I asked, "Is everyone clear on the rules?" With their eyes bright and their heads bobbing, we began.

"Who wants to start?" Tom asked with an encouraging, playful smile. Then, to our amazement, Chloe volunteered.

Chloe's youthful nervous laugh put everyone at ease and she began, "I want to talk about how Billy bothers me."

"Go right ahead," I encouraged.

"Billy, when you call me names or take my stuff and mess it up, I feel, well I'm not sure what I feel. I think it is . . . unimportant, like you don't care. Dr. Bev, what is the deeper feeling behind that?" she asked. Before I could answer, she guessed. "Inferiority, that's it!" Chloe said, with obvious pride in her genius.

"Exactly, you feel inferior," I replied.

"Yes, and I don't like it! It hurts my feelings, too, so I guess that would be trauma or pain," she added truthfully, while pointing to the chart. "I feel both inferior and hurt," she replied, with sadness in her voice.

"Billy, do you understand that you hurt Chloe with your words and actions?" Tom asked. Billy looked at Chloe curiously, nodding his head in assent. "I think so," he said, as he acted uncomfortable and searched for words. However, he actually did an amazing job for a six-year-old boy. "I don't want her to feel bad, but she tries to control me too much 'cause she's older, and I get mad. It's not fair, and the only thing I know to do is call her names or hit her."

"I understand that," Tom said. "But can you see that if you get mad, it doesn't make anything better?"

"Yeah," Billy answered still nodding his head up and down.

"Good."

Then Billy asked, "Can I have my turn now?"

"Sure."

"Chloe, when you boss me, call me names, and take over the TV remote all the time, I feel . . ." Billy pointed to his drawing and said, "put down."

"Great work finding the deeper emotion, Billy," Tom cheered. "It seems you both have been putting each other down and hurting each other's feelings. Do you know how the other person feels now?" Both Chloe and Billy's heads were bobbing.

"Do you think this understanding could change the way you act with each other? Can you find a better way to handle this?" Tom inquired.

"Sometimes, but sometimes I just want to watch what I want to watch," was Billy's honest childlike answer. His candor made us all laugh, and it was a nice break from the seriousness of the moment.

Then Billy and Chloe got more somber. "Really, I will try not to boss Billy too much, and share more stuff with him. He's not really a moron or an idiot. I'm sorry I said that, Billy," Chloe said, as she grinned at him on the sofa.

Obviously moved by Chloe's innocent candor, Billy volunteered, "I'll try to share with you too. You're not an idiot either." He grinned and they both giggled, partly because they felt self-conscious, and partly because they really did care about one another. This levity paved the way for their parents to share.

Amy went next, trying to focus while giggling. She sobered up and peered intently at the floor as she began to share. "Bill, when you get really grouchy and distant with the family, I feel fear. I never realized this before we came to counseling, but I'm afraid that the kids will feel about you the way you feel about your father." We could tell that Amy was hesitant to arouse Bill's anger, but she felt more comfortable with two therapists in the room.

Bill seemed ready to be reactive, but he had learned earlier that criticism, whether real or perceived, triggered his childhood wounds from his father. He actually stayed calm, mindful, and intentional, as we could see him struggle to bite his tongue.

"Bill, is this what you want? Do you want Amy to be afraid?" Tom asked, watching his face for clues to his mood. His big brown eyes registered pain and new understanding.

"No," Bill said, with obvious sincerity. "I don't want her to be afraid, and I surely don't want my kids to feel about me the way I feel about Grandpa." The whole idea of an unhealthy generational pattern caused Bill to get emotional and we could see tears form in the corners of his eyes. Chloe and Billy were awed and so silent that you could hear a pin drop. They had rarely seen the tender, vulnerable side of their father and they seemed to want to take it all in.

Amy, moved by Bill's candor and emotion, patted him on the shoulder. Bill then said softly, "I don't want our kids to resent me." He paused, trying to hold in his emotions, and we could tell that he was recollecting the pain he felt from his own father. He continued with conviction, "I'll do whatever it takes to make sure this doesn't happen to our family." By then, tears of gratitude had formed in Amy's eyes. Chloe cried too, and Billy sat perfectly still. Then it was Bill's turn to do the GIFT exercise.

We could tell that Bill had reached his emotional quota and wanted to bow out, but his family had already set such a good example for him that he couldn't refuse. After he composed himself, he said, "Amy, when you correct me or go behind my back in disciplining the kids I feel . . ." he paused for a few minutes to determine the root of his anger. We could see that he was struggling. Men have a hard time identifying the primary emotion underneath their anger. Unfortunately, anger gives men a false sense of power, and talking of guilt, inferiority, fear, or hurt makes them feel weak and vulnerable. We believe that a real man doesn't hide behind his anger; he shares his vulnerability, especially with those he loves.

Tom provided a nudge for Bill by repeating the acronym. Pointing to the chart, he said, "Guilt, Inferiority, Fear . . ."

"Inferiority!" Bill interrupted. "I feel inferior, like Amy thinks I'm a bad dad, and I also feel hurt that Amy does not trust my motives."

"Excellent job!" Tom commended.

Amy was shocked, as the insight light bulb went off in her head. "Bill, I never thought that you felt put down. You certainly never showed it! You actually bullied me. I don't want you to feel inferior. In fact, I want just the opposite. I guess my criticism did not help the situation. It actually hurt it," Amy softly confessed. The children were still reverent statues, absorbing the honesty and healing in the room. Amy's vulnerability obviously softened Bill.

"If we were at home, she never would have admitted all this stuff," Bill said teasingly. Once again, laughter lightened up the room and Amy teased back, "Yes, I would. It just helped to have a little coaching from the Relationship Doctors." We all continued to laugh.

"Bill, I know you love the kids," Amy continued, "but it would help for you to learn to break some bad habits you learned from your father. I'm sorry for the control and criticism. I think we both were hurting each other, and now that we know that, we can stop. I want to commit to changing my critical behavior."

"You all did such great work in being honest and understanding each other's deeper feelings. I'm proud of you for really hearing each other and sharing from your heart. Can we all take a second and list again the changes you are going to make and why?" Tom asked.

Amy repeated, "I will work on my criticism because I know it hurts Bill."

"I'm going to be mindful of my grouchiness and act intentionally so that I don't repeat my dad's mistakes," Bill said.

"I don't want Billy to feel put down so I'll try to share more," chimed Chloe.

Billy offered, "I will try to not call Chloe names so I don't hurt her feelings."

"You all have done an excellent job with the GIFT exercise. Do you think you can try this at home when you get angry with each other in the future?" Tom questioned.

"We'll sure try, right guys?" Amy asked, smiling at the children.

We all soaked up this holy moment, as this wonderful family grew immeasurably.

The GIFT exercise created a paradigm shift for the Smiths. They began to look underneath their anger at what was really going on within themselves and each other. Not only did their power struggles decrease, but they resolved them in a more healthy, godly manner.

What about you? Can you identify your family power struggles? Here is some homework that can help.

Healing Homework

- List the top issues you fight about as a couple and as a family.
- List three ways that you can work toward the middle attitudinally and behaviorally concerning issues that you are polarized about.
- Discuss mindfulness, intentionality, and sacrifice as a family and list practical ways you can do these things for each other.
- Practice using the GIFT exercise on the issues in your family power struggle.
- Have a family forum and allow all the children to practice the GIFT exercise as well.

Chapter Nine

Family Storms Are Inevitable

*W*e could hear it raging outside like a flood: a terrible spring storm. They are notorious for wreaking havoc on the budding southern countryside. The wind kicked up, forcefully pulling trees up by the roots. Some of these trees were a hundred years old, so the root systems were over eight feet in diameter. The ancient oaks plunged to the ground taking down power lines with their branches and pulling up concrete sidewalks with their great roots. One woman was severely injured across town, when a mighty maple pummeled her SUV while she drove to pick up her children from school. Hundreds of people lost power. We were lucky that the power outages missed us this time. It had been a week of storms and this one felt like it was not going to end any time soon!

As Tom and I sat holding our breath for fear we would lose electricity, we could hear loud thuds on the roof. We looked out in the yard and could see golf-ball sized hail coming down. We often see clients in our home, especially when the weather is bad, so we paused for a minute to make sure we had parked our cars in the garage when we came home to finish our workday. Both of us breathed a sigh of relief when we realized our vehicles were secure. Tom looked out into the yard that he had just seeded and saw that the torrential rains were washing the seeds away. What the water didn't damage, the hail finished off.

"So much for a plush green lawn this summer," he lamented.

Just then I remembered my garden. I rushed to the window on the side of the house just in time to see a young skinny birch topple over right in the center of my glorious garden. The seedlings I had nurtured, the zinnias and marigolds I had babied were all washed away. The gardenias and camellias were taking a brutal beating and the freshly planted geraniums were flattened! There was nothing we could do but wait. So we waited and waited and it stormed and stormed.

We could hear the ambulances going by, no doubt rescuing stranded drivers or rushing to the scenes of fender benders or worse accidents. We wondered if our clients could make it to our home office and tried to calculate the damage done by this mean monsoon. It was not the first storm to ravage our community this season and it would not be the last.

While we waited for the torrent to relent and prayed for our clients' safe travel to our home office, we began to discuss how storms are inevitable and happen to all of us. Because we have ministered to thousands of families over the past two and a half decades, we believe that family storms can be the most painful. They can do the worst kind of damage because the ones we love can trigger us and wound us like no one else, and we can do likewise to them. These inevitable family storms can be difficult to survive.

We thought about various clients who had recently experienced storms. John and Kristen were besieged by a family storm when they found out that 15-year-old Johnny was using drugs. As the storm raged, he got in trouble with the police and was expelled from school. They wondered what had happened. They had raised Johnny with Christian principles, so how could this be? As the wind of rebellion and the hail of pain ravaged them, John realized that he had worked too much, making work an idol. He had also pushed his laidback son to be as driven as he was. John and Kristen would fight because John never praised Johnny's bent toward music. He wanted Johnny to be more like him and be interested in business and accounting. Johnny was now paying him back in a passive-aggressive storm of rebellion.

Tammy and Don were being barraged by the wind and hail of shame as they found out that little Erica was caught cheating and was in danger of failing the sixth grade. Tammy and Don realized that the tension in their marriage had left little time to spend with Erica. She was going to get their attention—but in a negative manner.

Paul and Chris were experiencing a storm when their eight-year-old son, Josh, threw a rock on the playground and hit another child in the head, injuring him badly. They knew that Josh's anger was escalating but they kept their heads in the sand, thinking it was just a phase he was going through. While the storm raged on, they wondered when it would end and what would be left in the wake of its destruction.

All of these families had one commonality: They were hurting at the hands of those they loved. They were in the midst of great family storms. It seems that no matter how you prepare, and what you do to stop them, storms will inevitably come.

Our clients, the Smith family, finally arrived, soaked by the downpour and bombarded by the onslaught of hail. Bill and Amy shook their saturated umbrellas and jackets on the porch and stepped inside out of the storm. Billy and Chloe stomped in the large puddles that formed on the cement, splashing each other mercilessly. They wielded their yellow rain slickers like swords outside the door in an effort to get dry. Billy was holding two balls of hail in his hands and inspecting them as he entered. Both he and Chloe were talking over each other about the exciting adventure they'd had on the way to our place. They had stopped under an awning at a service station to allow the hail to pass and to protect the family car. But the storm they had just escaped was not nearly as bad as the one they had just been through as a family.

We had not seen the Smiths for two and a half months. In that time, the kids had had spring break from school and the family had gone camping in the mountains. They returned home to the news that Bill's dad had died of a heart attack. Bill went into a funk and retreated to his dungeon, and had hardly left it ever since.

True to form, Bill's mom and brothers left him out of the funeral arrangements and this crushed him. It was just one more instance in a lifetime of rejection that he had suffered at the hands of those he loved and who were supposed to love him. Bill realized that now he would never get his father's approval and affirmation, and the rejection of his family would continue even after his father's death. This realization was almost too much for him to bear. The messages of his wounds—*you're not good enough, you'll never get the blessing*—echoed in his soul as he resorted to his old adaptation: distance and withdrawal. It was a storm that he felt he could not handle anymore.

"It's been hard since Bill's dad passed away. Bill has had a hard time. He's been really depressed," Amy said, struggling for words, obviously trying not to upset Bill, but wanting us to know the truth.

"Dad's been kind of grouchy," Chloe offered impulsively, unable to restrain her ADHD tendency to blurt out whatever was on her mind. "He's back in his dungeon again and we've had no pancakes on Saturday either since Grandpa died. We're kind of sad about Grandpa's death too, but we really didn't know him that well."

Bill looked beleaguered and guilty and only offered a shrug in his defense.

"Bill, how are you doing with all of this?" Tom asked.

"It's hit me so hard. I don't understand. My dad and I were never close. I've tried not to be grouchy and distant but I guess I can't help it." Bill's large brown eyes looked sad as he spoke.

"You're grieving," Tom said gently. "It's okay to be sad and depressed when you grieve. You are sad for what you lost with your dad, and more importantly, you are sad for what you never had." Something in Tom's words released a floodgate of emotion in Bill and he started to cry. Everyone was surprised at how emotional he was. Embarrassed, he tried to control himself, but the emotion kept coming. The rest of the family was reverent and respectful of his pain.

"It's good to cry when you lose someone or something. Tears have a way of washing the soul," Tom encouraged.

Wiping his eyes, Bill said, "It may be good to be sad and cry, but it's not good to take it out on everyone else."

"You're right," I said, praising him for his insight and candor. "That's wise of you and shows that you have grown."

"I don't feel like I've grown at all. I feel like I've gone backward. I don't understand. We were doing so well, and this happened and now everything bothers me again. I don't like to be around people and I know this hurts my family. I just want to stay to myself. It seems that I've lost all of the ground that I had gained," he shared honestly while looking at Chloe and Billy.

Chloe's impulsivity got the best of her again and she honestly blurted out, "Yeah, and we miss our pancakes on the weekends!"

"They all want pancakes," I said softly with compassion, "but they want the pancake-maker more. They miss you, Bill, and they all want their daddy back."

"What happened? How could one thing like this ruin all the work I did?"

"It's not ruined, Bill. It's just a storm," I answered. "Grief and loss can create terrible hail that pounds our hearts and souls. You lost your father but you also lost the dream of ever having a dad. It was hard for me, too, when I buried my mother along with the hope of having her love and care. Another reason for your recent setback is spending time with your mother and brothers. Being around family can bring back echoes of the messages of the soul wounds they have inflicted upon you in the past. You can often feel just as miserable as you did as a child, which is why family gatherings can be difficult, and funerals even more treacherous. Unfortunately, because you were swept away by the waters of rejection, you went back to your old adaptation and ran to your dungeon. You then felt like you were right back where you started. But you're not. You have only been through a storm, and the Lord has been there with you and He will direct your path through it."

I could see that this information gave Amy and the kids a better understanding of Bill's recent behavior, because they looked calmer and more compassionate toward Bill. It also helped Bill to have more mercy on himself, and hope for the future.

"So you mean I'm not a lost cause?"

"No, there are no lost causes in the kingdom of God."

"Then how can we get out of this pit?" Bill asked.

"We are so glad you asked. There is a way out, a way of hope through the storms of life. It is a kind of survival guide and we'd love to share it with you. Are you ready for a story?" I asked. By now, the Smiths were used to our stories and enjoyed them, so they nodded their heads in affirmation. Chloe grabbed the soft afghan on the back of the sofa and covered her and her mom's laps in preparation for our narrative.

"This is a good one. It's about a really wise man who lived thousands of years ago. He really knew what storms were all about and how to help people through them. This wise man was none other than the Old Testament prophet Isaiah," I said and began the saga.

We shared with the Smith family an abbreviated version of the story we are about to tell you. It has helped countless families find their way out of the storm and perhaps it can help you. So grab an afghan and settle in for a tale of hope.

FAMILIES NEED HOPE

What every family needs in the middle of the storm is hope. But, in the gales of life, hope is hard to find. When prayers seem to go unanswered, or situations seem too hard to bear, our humanity can get the best of us. We feel cheated, as if God is holding out on us or is not taking care of us. Old messages haunt our souls as we feel like hope eludes us.

Those of us who have suffered from a great many soul wounds take storms very hard. Adult children from really dysfunctional families have more depression, anxiety, lower self-esteem, and generally poorer coping mechanisms than those people who were not as wounded.[1] Because of this, storms tend to bowl us over and we can drift from the Lord. The very thing we need is closeness with the Almighty, but the messages of our soul wounds tell us that He cannot be trusted either. We believe He, just like our perpetrating parents or family members, has forgotten us as well. Nothing could be further from the truth, but these messages have been with us for a long time and have a very powerful pull on our souls. And so we drift, unintentionally and sometimes intentionally, and all the while the Lord desires closeness with us. He even uses the events of our lives to hem us in until we look upward and see that He is still on the throne. He did this in Isaiah's day as well.

THE WISDOM OF A SAGE

Our story begins in Judah, which was then in the land of southern Israel. King Uzziah, a godly ruler, had died, leaving Judah grieving and vulnerable. Israel's future was uncertain and without a godly leader, they began to turn toward sin. Isaiah's message counseled them against their sin and idolatry and, as you can imagine, was very unpopular. He warned Judah not to make unhealthy alliances with Assyria, Moab,

Babylon, and many other ungodly forces, yet they struggled. When tragedy hits, we too can make unhealthy alliances. We believe the messages of our soul wounds and act in ways that are ungodly and unhealthy, all the while moving further and further away from the Lord, like Judah.

For 39 chapters, Isaiah warned his people about their sin and distance from God, but they did not hear. The great prophet exhorted Judah that the Lord would be their help and hope in the storm, but still they distanced themselves.

The remaining 27 chapters of Isaiah contain some of the most beautiful and intimate word pictures of God calling His own to Himself. It is the essence of the gospel itself, as God reminds His people that He has created them, sustained them, called them back to relationship with Him alone, and assured them that He would never abandon them. He tells them again that He will never leave them, and asks them in this context to return, repent, renew their relationship with Him, and rejoice in His continual and loving care for His chosen people. This is the key to healing for us as well, as we'll discuss in the next chapter.

Chapter Ten

The Four R's of Healing:
Return, Repent,
Renew, Rejoice

*I*saiah gave the people of Judah (and us) four steps to healing life's storms. In following these steps, we can heal our souls and the souls of other family members as well. Lucky for us, they all start with the letter R, creating a memorable alliteration. We call these steps the Four R's of Healing.

We use Isaiah's four steps of healing with families to help them deal with their soul wounds and the ensuing storms that can trouble them as a result. Again, the healing steps detailed in the book of Isaiah are: Return, Repent, Renew, and Rejoice. These are a pathway out of pain and suffering for individuals, couples, and families alike. Let's look at each step further.

Step 1: Return

Like many of us when family storms hit, Bill Smith found himself once again believing the messages of his soul wounds. He heard painful messages like *you are not good enough and you will never get your parents' blessing* echo in his psyche. So, he found himself distancing from the Lord. Pain has a way of haunting us with the unhealthy messages from the past and making us revisit the very wounds that caused these messages. When this happens we, like Bill, can distance ourselves from the Lord. Perhaps this is because the pain is so familiar. After all, we have worn it like a tattered shawl most of our lives. Or maybe it is because we start to doubt our soul-healing Savior and even blame Him for not protecting us from the storm. It is the very antithesis of what we should do, but the psyche betrays our attempts toward health and bathes us in familiar pain. You may know what we are talking about here.

The Lord will forever call us to return to Him when we are wayward, just as He did in Isaiah's day. The people of Judah were in a storm of grief, and in their pain they drifted from the Lord. Isaiah's famous words "Here am I. Send me!" (Isaiah 6:8) were an answer to God's call to move his people to return to God. "Many peoples will come and say, 'Come, let us go up to the mountain of the LORD, to the house of the God of Jacob. He will teach us his ways, so that we may walk in his paths'"(Isaiah 2:3). But they did not hear the words of the prophet. Often, we don't hear the Lord calling us to return either; this may be because the messages of our soul wounds drown Him out.

In order to stop our distancing and return to the Lord in times of storm, we must challenge the messages by looking at where they come from. Most of the time, this will be our soul wounds. The Lord wants to heal our wounds, but we will need to move toward Him, not away, in order to let this happen. Isaiah's words to Judah apply to us today: "Yet the Lord longs to be gracious to you; he rises to show you compassion. For the Lord is a God of justice. Blessed are all who wait for him!" (Isaiah 30:18). God extends His gracious hand to us in our distance and pain and tells us to weep no more, that He will be gracious when we cry for help. As soon as He hears, He will answer us. Even though we have the bread of adversity and the water of affliction (which we call soul wounds), the Lord will be hidden no more and again we will hear His voice behind us telling us how to walk in His ways (Isaiah 30:19–21).

Even after repeated urgings to return to the Lord, the people of
Judah still resisted. Like many of us, they continued to drift. Believing the unhealthy messages of our soul wounds leads to unhealthy
adaptations—those behaviors we engage in as a result of the wounds. We
may rage, try too hard to control or fix the situation, caretake exces-
sively, shut down, or give up. These adaptations do not heal the wounds;
they further reinforce them. Adaptive behaviors can become habituated
and we turn to them by default, as the old brain takes over and we become enslaved to unhealthy patterns.

In returning to the Lord, we will have to surrender our adaptations
to Him. He is waiting for us to come to relinquish these adaptations
when he says through his prophet, "Do you not know? Have you not
heard? The Lord is the everlasting God, the Creator of the ends of the
earth. He will not grow tired or weary, and his understanding no one can
fathom. He gives strength to the weary and increases power to the weak.
But those who hope in the Lord will renew their strength. They will
soar on wings like eagles; they will run and not grow weary, they will
walk and not be faint" (Isaiah 40:28–29, 31).

Even as I write these words, I (Bev) am moved to tears. This verse
has so often been a beacon in the wilderness of my childhood pain when
I have distanced from the Lord in my unhealthy adaptations. Like
Judah, I have resisted the Lord's call to return and tried to go it alone.
Unfortunately, when adaptations don't work we often turn to worse be-
haviors. We then move to indulgences.

INDULGENCES

Indulgences are those things we do when even adaptations aren't enough.
We indulge in unhealthy behaviors to mask our hurt or stop the pain.
We falsely think that indulgences can fix our situation, but they only
make it worse. Addictions are a chief form of indulgence, but too much

food, alcohol, work, busyness, and hiding can perpetuate the storm as well.

While the Lord has done a great deal to heal me over the years, in times of great storms, I can still revert to my old familiar indulgence of busyness. As a child when my mother would scream and stomp around the house like a tyrant, (no doubt an adaptation or indulgence from her own painful childhood), I would get busy and start cleaning. She liked for us to clean, and I learned early that if I cleaned, she would not get as angry with me. When she would start a rant, I would grab a sponge and begin to scrub the floors or wash the walls. Sometimes this would cause her wrath toward me to decrease. Because of this, I developed a bad habit of getting too busy when storms would hit. While I got a lot done, I would not let myself feel the pain that was necessary to heal. The outcome is guilt, depression, and despair—a sad, unhealthy result.

THE RESULT

The result of our unhealthy indulgences is that they put us right back where we started, believing the messages of our soul wounds again! Here is how this harmful cycle goes. The inevitable storm hits, we feel the pain of that storm and we are haunted by the injurious messages of our soul wounds. We then adapt with our detrimental behaviors, and when that doesn't work, we indulge. These indulgences cause us to feel terrible about ourselves and there we are again, believing the unhealthy messages. This is not the result we were looking for and it is a damaging trap. The only way out is to return to the Lord, surrender our adaptations, and hand over our indulgences. Even in our sin and indulgent behaviors the Lord tells us through Isaiah, "Do not be afraid, O Jacob, my servant, Jeshurun, whom I have chosen. For I will pour water on the thirsty land and streams on the dry ground" (Isaiah 44:2b–3a). The Lord is waiting for us to return to Him for His help in the storms of life.

RETURN TO YOUR FIRST LOVE

To return means to come back to a former place, position, or state. We are to come back to our first love, to a confident faith, to a romance with the Lord. Sometimes God even uses personal crises to get our attention. This is what happened in Isaiah's day. King Uzziah's death marked the end of a godly era and the people were fearful and uncertain of the future. The Lord used Isaiah to get His children's attention. He uses our personal storms to get our attention as well, as He calls us closer to Him. *The Soul Care Bible* says, "God is the master of the unexpected invasion, and he will use any tool at hand when he breaks through a person's defenses. The walls of arguments, excuses, and ignorance that often stand between people and God crumble under God's persistent grace. His purpose is neither to defeat nor conquer. He wants to set us free. He knows that everything we use to try to keep God out actually only keeps us imprisoned within."[1] The Lord desires for us to come back to him and be set free from the imprisonment of our unhealthy behaviors.

No matter what we have done in our wayward state, God wants us to return. Isaiah's beautiful words say, " 'Come now, let us reason together,' says the Lord. 'Though your sins are like scarlet, they shall be as white as snow' " (Isaiah 1:18).

Step 2: Repent

Step two on this journey is to repent of the unhealthy ways in which we tried to survive the storm. To repent is to feel regretful or contrite for past conduct. It is to have sorrow and remorse for the past and therefore turn away from our unhealthy, ungodly ways. Striving in our own flesh leads to pain. Isaiah tells us, "In repentance and rest is your salvation, in quietness and trust is your strength" (Isaiah 30:15).

Like many of us, the people of Judah resisted the message of Isaiah to repent. Feeling like the Lord had let them down, they took matters into their own hands. They said, "Lord, I don't trust you in the storm so I am going to handle things myself." We, too, can do this when we feel that the Lord has abandoned us and we attempt to trust in ourselves and not God. Like Judah, we are "ever hearing, but never understanding . . . ever seeing, but never perceiving" (Isaiah 6:9). God's patience ran thin as He told Isaiah to deliver this message: "Make the heart of this people calloused; make their ears dull and close their eyes. Otherwise they might see with their eyes, hear with their ears, understand with their hearts, and turn and be healed"(Isaiah 6:10).

I have to be honest here. This passage scared me when I was a new, immature Christian. I did not want to be like the people of Judah who were hardened and calloused. I did not want God's patience, loving-kindness, and mercy for me to grow faint. But, because of the many soul wounds from my childhood, the messages haunted me in times of storm and pushed me toward self instead of toward God. I used to think that if things were going to get better in my life, *I* had to provide the remedy. I had trouble trusting God and faith was very difficult for me. I now know that adult children of abuse and dysfunction have a harder time with faith. We have difficulty seeing the positive side of trials. Having been wounded by those we love, we tend to put our wounding parent's face on the Lord and see Him as a wounder as well.

BEV'S STORY

Many of my childhood storms were ushered in by my mother's emotional and physical abuse. She once exploded at us for coloring and hiding Easter eggs. It was my feeble attempt to have fun in that painful house. My mother awoke from one of her famous eight-hour naps (in her untreated depressive stupor she often slept the days away) to find us hiding eggs in the yard. She stormed to the front porch and yelled, "You kids get over here! Eggs are food not play toys," she bellowed with her hands firmly planted on her wide hips. She promptly ordered us inside and she took all of our beautiful egg creations and threw them against the wall, creating a miserable mess.

"Now clean this all up," she ordered. "This will teach you to play with food. Food is expensive. You'll learn never to waste it again!"

We cleaned everything up as we cried because our celebration had come to such a horrible end. I was devastated and furious, but I dared not let any of my anger show for fear of incurring even more of my mother's monstrous wrath. But that did not stop me from being passive-aggressive. Since I could not be a hurler, I defaulted to the hider position, and secretly kept one egg. It was my beautiful golden-yellow masterpiece. I hid it in my jacket in protest of my mother's evil rant. When she left for work at the local hotel and pub, I continued to hide the golden egg, giving my siblings great joy and feeling like I had gained some victory over my abuser.

While this passive-aggressive act may have saved our Easter celebration and given us a modicum of joy in the Sheol that was our home, it unfortunately set up a pattern whereby I felt like I had to take matters into my own hands. When the frequent storms of abuse deluged our home, I would resort to my own plans and developed an unhealthy belief that I could trust no one but myself. This often stood in the way of my trusting the Lord in times of trouble. I thought that if I could not trust my own mother who was supposed to love me more than anyone on earth, then how was I going to trust a supreme being that I could not even see. I doubted my Creator. Like the people of Judah, I quarreled with my Maker.

Isaiah told his people, "Woe to him who quarrels with his Maker. . . . Does the clay say to the potter, 'What are you making?' "

(Isaiah 45:9). Well, if you were me years ago, the answer would unfortunately be yes. I constantly argued with my Maker about the storms I was experiencing, which led me to establish a pattern of stubborn self-protection as a result. But true to God's character, He called His children to repentance and He called me to His bosom as well. He said, "It is I who made the earth and created mankind upon it. My own hands stretched out the heavens; I marshaled their starry hosts. . . . I will make all his ways straight" (Isaiah 45:12–13).

I have read this passage many times in my years with the Lord, mostly when we are having a tug of war over my life's circumstances. I would tell Him that I wanted things my way, and He would call me to repentance and tell me He was going to do things His way. I have learned over the years that it is fruitless and even painful to play tug-of-war with the Lord. He is the one who made the world and put the stars in place. Arguing with Him is futile. We all know that He will inevitably win, so the only way to be peaceful and healthy is to repent.

Perhaps you, like me, have suffered pain at the hands of those who were supposed to cherish you. Maybe you were wounded by the anger of a parent, the betrayal of a spouse, or the ungodly choices of a beloved child that caused you horrific hurt. In your unhealthy adaptations, you felt like you could not trust the Lord, so you went it alone and in your flesh tried to fix what only the Lord can repair. There is hope in repentance. The Lord tells us that He can help us with our unhealthy behaviors. He reminds me regularly through His prophet Isaiah that he formed me in the womb to be His servant (Isaiah 49:5), and has called me by name (Isaiah 45:3). He is the one who blots out our transgressions for our own sake and remembers our sins no more (Isaiah 43:25). He has swept away our offenses like a cloud and our sins like the morning mist. The Lord asks us to return to Him for He has redeemed us (Isaiah 44:22).

CONFESSION

In your repentance, you can do what Isaiah called his people to do: Confess your unhealthy adaptations and sinful indulgences to the Lord. Surrender your unhealthy self-protection. Lay down your alliances and trust in men, and allow Him to heal and forgive. First John 1:9 says, "If we confess our sins, He is faithful and just and will forgive us our sins and purify us from all unrighteousness" (NKJV). His redemption ransomed us and set us free from sin and heals our soul wounds again and again, if we repent.

For the first 40 chapters of the book, Isaiah called God's people to repentance and redemption. The prophet then changed his message to one of hope, renewal, and restoration. The next step, then, is to renew.

Step 3: Renew and Restore

Renew means to give something back to its proper place or owner or return someone to a previous office or rank. When life's storms hit and we stop trusting the Lord, we inadvertently forfeit our position and rank as a son or daughter of the King. I am ashamed to admit that when I would bury myself in my own self-protective plans, I would often forget that I was a child of the Most High God who could do all things. I would get so busy with my own futile fleshly strategies that I would actually forget that it is the Lord who will renew me and restore me to my proper place and position. That place is as His daughter embodied with *His* power, not mine.

Restore means to replace something that is no longer useful. After we repent, we find that our unhealthy behaviors are no longer useful. We need to replace them with new healthy behaviors that will honor the Lord and lead us out of the storm. It also means to reaffirm a promise or commitment, or to make something new again. The Lord longs to make us new again just as He did for the children of southern Israel. The first part of the step toward renewal and restoration is to ask the Lord to heal you.

Ask the Lord to Heal You

In your renewal and restoration, ask the Lord to heal the soul wounds that lead to the unhealthy adaptations and indulgences that make you distance from the Lord and cause you to forfeit your position and place with Him. The Lord used Isaiah to tell us, "Fear not, for I have redeemed you; I have summoned you by name; you are mine. When you pass through the waters, I will be with you; and when you pass through the rivers, they will not sweep over you. When you walk through the fire, you will not be burned; the flames will not set you ablaze. For I am the Lord, your God. . . . You are precious and honored in my sight . . . Do not be afraid, for I am with you; Forget the former things; do not dwell on the past. See, I am doing a new thing!" (Isaiah 43:1b–5, 18–19a).

I love the words of this wise ancient scribe. On the path to renewal and restoration, I walked though the waters of abuse and did not drown. I journeyed through the fires of pain and did not get burned. Even now the Lord continues to protect and heal me and enables me not to dwell on my painful past and to see that He is "doing a new thing" in me daily.

Not dwelling on the past can be difficult, especially when the old brain betrays you. Tom and I still feel shame and sadness for the unhealthy behaviors we tried in the storms of life. We have had to grieve about our painful pasts and the harmful, and even sinful, behaviors that resulted from them. The people of Judah also had to grieve over their distance and sin. Fortunately, there is no better place to go in our regret than to the Lord. He, after all, was a man of sorrows familiar with grief (Isaiah 53:3).

Grieve Your Losses

The next step toward renewal and restoration leads you to grieve your losses. This brings us to healing premise #5:

HEALING PREMISE #5:
Grief is an important and necessary part of true healing.

Grieving can be one of the most painful processes you will undertake. It certainly was difficult for me. I felt that I had experienced so much hurt in my life that I did not want to feel any more. It was not a coincidence that I wrote this section of the book during Passion Week. This time of year, I am always reminded of the pain, humiliation, and grief that our innocent Savior suffered for my transgressions. Isaiah 53:7 says, "He was oppressed and afflicted, yet he did not open his mouth." This unselfish redemptive act continues to give me motivation to swim through the waters of sorrow and grief in an effort to be renewed and restored.

Just as God was for the children of Israel, He will be ever present in our pain. "In the time of my favor I will answer you, and in the day of salvation I will help you; I will keep you and will make you to be a covenant for the people, to restore the land and to reassign its desolate inheritances, to say to the captives, 'Come out' and to those in darkness, 'Be free'" (Isaiah 49:8b–9a). The Lord has renewed His covenant with me, and set me free from my own self-protective plans each time I distance from Him. He will do the same for you as you renew.

Change Your Behavior

Renewal and restoration are wonderful, but they will not be effective if your behavior does not change as a result. We have said before, "If nothing changes, nothing changes." Taking the step of renewal means forgetting the past with all of its fleshly behaviors and asking the Lord to teach us new ones. Instead of getting reactive, try intentionality. Rather than distancing, stay present and tell others how you feel. Replace excessive caretaking with balanced love and healthy detachment, which will prevent destructive enabling. Isaiah 48:17b says, "I am the Lord your God, who teaches you what is best for you, who directs you in the way you should go." Listen to Him as He teaches you new behaviors to replace the old useless ones. You will then be truly renewed and restored.

Step 4: Rejoice

The last step out of the storm is the best one. It is to rejoice and claim your healing and be thankful for it. To rejoice means to celebrate or express joy. Celebrate that the Lord has seen your distress and your storm is now over. Delight in the fact that He has a divine destiny for you, your spouse, and your entire family, and He will use this very storm to bring it about.

As our story of ancient Israel closes, we see that the people in Isaiah's day could also rejoice that the time of distance from their God was past. More than once I, too, have had cause to rejoice after the storm. I continue to rejoice that He has brought me out so many times and will go on healing the shame and disgrace of my past pain. For years I carried deep within my soul the shame of being an abused child. I was afraid to share my testimony because I felt the embarrassment of coming from such a troubled past. I was afraid people would think it was my fault or that somehow I was defective in some way. Those of you who have come from similar backgrounds know the shame and fear I speak of.

Over the years, the Lord has shown me that He uses the pain of our past and the storms of life to grow us and prepare us for his divine destiny for our lives. He did the same for his children in Isaiah's day. He tells us, "Do not be afraid . . . Do not fear disgrace; you will not be humiliated. You will forget the shame of your youth . . . The Lord will call you back . . . For a brief moment I abandoned you, but with deep compassion I will bring you back . . . my unfailing love for you will not be shaken nor my covenant of peace be removed, says the Lord" (Isaiah 54:4, 6–7, 10). What great news! We can rejoice that the Lord heals the shame of our past pain and has a great plan for our future after the storm.

The Lord through Isaiah told his people to build up their roads and remove the obstacles out of the way (Isaiah 57:14). This translates that He will help us clear out the path of our storms and make way for the great things He will do with us as a result. The Lord will guide us always and satisfy our needs in a sun-scorched land and will strengthen our frame. We will be like a watered garden and a spring whose waters never fail (Isaiah 58:11).

After a terrible southern spring storm, I am always amazed at how calm, peaceful, and beautiful everything looks. All you can see for miles is a cloudless Carolina blue sky; there is a freshness in the air that is unmistakable. It is as if the storm has purged us of our dross. Family storms can do the same thing for you if you will let them. They can purify us and prepare us for the newness of God's work in our lives.

On a plaque in my office is a quote by Patty Perricone that says, "Life isn't about waiting for the storm to pass. It's about learning to dance in the rain." These four steps that the wise prophet Isaiah encouraged his people to take can help you, too, learn to dance in the rain. And when you do you will be a "crown of splendor in the Lord's hand, a royal diadem in the hand of your God" (Isaiah 62:3).

This is the story of returning, repenting, renewing, and rejoicing

that we told the Smith family. It encouraged them to move toward healing the damage of the great storm they had just experienced. We pray
that it will encourage you as well.

Healing Homework

~ Below you will see a list of the Four R's of Healing. Scriptures
and sub-steps are also listed. Read each step and the correlating
scripture. Then write your reactions, comments, insight, and
prayers in the space available underneath.

~ Go through each step and read the Scriptures as a devotional or
Bible study for you and your family. Have each family member
complete the steps and write the prayers. If they are too young
to write, have them dictate to an older sibling or parent.

~ Share the prayers with one another during your devotional
time; write the prayers down and pray them for each other
regularly. Make sure you write praise reports of these answered prayers and the date in which the answer came.
Seeing that the Lord answers our prayers for healing encourages everyone.

The Four R's of Healing the Soul

Step 1. Return to the Lord and the first love you had when you met
Him, to the ways of a confident faith, to a romance with God.
Isaiah 1:25–26, Isaiah 2:3

Message: What is the message of fear that ensnares you and keeps
you from being the person the Lord wants you to be?

Wound: Where did the message come from? What happened in your life that wounded your soul? Ask the Lord for help in spotting your soul wounds.
Isaiah 30:18–21

Adaptation: What do you feel and do because of the message and the wound? Examples: Try too hard, give up, control, self-hate, caretake, distance from others and God.
Isaiah 40:27–31

Indulgence: What did you do to stop the pain, and to try to medicate your hurt or cover it up? What are the things you do when the adaptations do not work? These can be idols in your life. An idol is anything that you value more than you value the Lord; something that you think about more than thinking about the things of God. Examples: Romance novels, food, alcohol, work, Christian service, worry, victimization, socializing.
Isaiah 44:9–11

Result: What is the end result? How do you feel after all of this? Examples: Guilt, shame, depression, anxiety, hiding from love, looking for love in the wrong places.

Step 2. Repent of any way in which you took matters into your own hands and did not trust God to take care of you when you were afraid. Confess the flesh and the ways you controlled things.

   Isaiah 43:25, 51:11–16

Step 3. Renew and Restore your promise and commitment to God and His to you. Remember your position as a child of the Most High God.

   Ask the Lord to Heal You: **Isaiah 43:18–19, 53:5**

   Grieve (Find your tears): **Isaiah 53:3, 49:8–9, 13**

What's God's Truth? — How will this help?

   Change your behavior: List what things you will do differently as a result of this exercise and experience.

Step 4: Rejoice in the call He has for you, in your divine destiny, in how He is going to use your past pain to glorify Himself, and that He will heal your wounded soul over and over again.

   Isaiah 52:7, 61:1–4, 62:3

   Claim your healing and be thankful for it. Write a prayer of thanksgiving.

Chapter Eleven

Facing the Enemy: Changing the Messages of Satan in Your Family

*T*he Smith family sat spellbound as Tom and I finished our story of Isaiah and the people of Judah. We could tell by their faces that the news of God's renewal was helpful for them as they navigated through their family storm. Chloe perked up on the sofa between her parents, unable to contain her curiosity, and asked, "Why did it take so long for the people to turn to God?"

"Yeah," Billy added, "Mom says that that's really bad to do."

"You are absolutely right. That is awesome insight for someone so young," I said to Billy, as he beamed with pride. As was typical, Chloe chimed in to compete for the praise I was offering.

"Mom tells us about a lot of people in the Bible who didn't follow God when He first called them. Like Jonah and Lot," she reported, feverishly concentrating, trying to think of more.

"Very good, Chloe, you sure know a lot about the Bible!" I commended. Chloe then gave Billy a superior look that showed that she, too, was praiseworthy.

"It seems that from time to time all of us drift from God, especially when times are hard. He calls us back like He did the people of Judah, but often we resist. The Four R's of Healing will help all of you move closer when you have trouble hearing God calling you to Him," I told the Smiths.

"The steps are great," Amy added. "I plan on making them a part of our family devotions if Bill will help me."

"I plan on doing the exercise for myself and I'd be glad to do it as a family," Bill said. Amy was obviously pleased by his response, but seemed a bit hesitant. "Why is it so hard sometimes to follow the Lord's call?" Amy looked around the room at her family and continued. "I, well, we all, have trouble at times doing what the Lord wants us to do. We know that He loves us and has our best interests in mind. We learned this from you in counseling. But why is it so hard at times?"

"Quite honestly, Amy, I think that the answer lies not in *why* but in *whom*. Tom and I believe that it is Satan, the enemy of our souls that keeps us from getting closer to the Lord. Satan is waging a war against us, a war for the family, a war for our very souls. One of his chief weapons against us is reminding many of us of our past pain, making us hurt over and over again. Reliving this hurt causes us to feel hopeless, even cynical, and we start to believe that things will never change. But there is a way to stop him in his tracks and we will tell you how in our next meeting."

The Smiths left with the anticipation of doing the Four R's of Healing and learning about spiritual warfare in the family when they returned.

You, too, may have felt some of the same frustration that Amy Smith voiced. You gain some victory over dealing with your painful past, only to lose ground later. Tom and I have been there many times ourselves.

After almost three decades of working with hurting families, we have learned that you cannot ignore the power of the enemy of our souls and his evil plot against us.

THE ENEMY'S EVIL PLOT

Tom and I have never liked to hear people constantly talk about Satan. When we were newly married, we served in a church of some very emotionally unhealthy people who cast demons out of everything, including inanimate objects! They pushed deliverance on people in a fanatical manner and had many of them burn family heirlooms that they believed to be cursed. These naive Christians were imprisoned by fear and talked much more about the enemy than the Savior.

While we believe spiritual warfare and deliverance have their place in dealing with the enemy, too much focus on Satan can take the emphasis off of the real power to heal you which is the soul-healing love of Jesus Christ. There needs to be a balanced approach to spiritual warfare. Giving too much credit to Satan can be unhealthy, not to mention impotent. But not respecting his evil designs against us can also be unhealthy and can cause us to be ignorant of the war he is waging against us. Unfortunately, I know this plot all too well.

BEV'S STORY

You cannot grow up in a home like mine and miss seeing the devastating power of the devil at work. After my sister and I got saved in our little country church, our impassioned pastor would preach fiery sermons about the Prince of Darkness. I remember that I never liked it when he did that. I already had a lot of fear in my life from living with an abusive mother who could explode at any minute. Just hearing about Satan made it worse. Though I did not like hearing them, I could not help but believe that the stories about him were true. In fact, I could not help but believe that I was actually living them.

There was something disturbingly dark about my mother's behavior. A lot of it was mental illness, but there was more. My mother seemed to gain pleasure in punishing those who were weaker and more helpless. There was a menacing manner in the way she acted against my sister and me, particularly after we got saved and started going to church. She welcomed the fact that the people at church would take us kids off her hands on Sundays, but she seemed to be very upset that we actually liked what we heard and had started to believe their teachings.

"I sent you kids to church to get you out of my hair, not so that you would become fanatics," she would rant. As she stomped around the small shack we called home, all 250 pounds of her shook the damaged flooring beneath her feet, scaring us to death.

"Church is for holy rollers and snake handlers." Apparently, my mother had the misfortune of being dragged to a small country church where pew jumping and snake handling were prevalent. This was, no doubt, another of her many soul wounds.

"Do you really want to be like them?" She would bellow, "They are all crazy!"

Well, if that is not the pot calling the kettle black, then I don't know what is, I would think to myself as she raged. At the time, I did not understand why my mother was so upset about my allegiance to the church. It took years and a bachelor's degree in biblical literature to figure out that she felt threatened. I learned that my mother allowed the enemy to use her to try to discourage her children from the ways of the Lord. The reason she was so dead-set against the church was because she was being used as a pawn by Satan in a great spiritual war over my soul and the souls of my family. One of the enemy's greatest strategies is using family members against each other to their demise. Satan wanted to destroy my family, and he has set his sights on yours as well.

THE BATTLE FOR THE FAMILY

If Satan can break up a marriage, tempt a child to rebel, or make a father believe the negative messages of his soul wounds so that he provokes his children to wrath, then he can affect an entire clan for generations to come. Part of why the Smiths, and all of us, have trouble hanging on to our victory and reveling in our renewal is because the enemy has hatched a sinister scheme against families.

Our nation's families are under attack. Traditional marriage, once seen as a revered institution and a covenant to last a lifetime, has been minimized to a sentimental ceremony, or overlooked altogether. This is possibly because the divorce rate, though declining, still hovers around 33 percent in our country.[1] This means that a significant number of families sitting in our church pews at any given time are in peril. The marriage rate is dropping as singles are deciding to delay marriage or shying away from it all together. Many singles are choosing unhealthy options like nonmarried coparenting or cohabitation.[2] The gay marriage agenda and other liberal, nontraditional family styles threaten the continuation of family life as we know it. All are works of the enemy in his war on the family.

In order to fight this war, we all need to be aware of our adversary's strategies. Lucifer's chief strategy is to tell us lies. In fact, John 8:44 says that he is the father of lies. He tells mothers and fathers that they are ineffective, making them feel hopeless as parents. He tells sons and daughters that their parents are withholding the pleasures of this world, tempting them to rebel. He tells elderly grandparents that they are forgotten leftovers from another life, causing them to feel depressed and forlorn. These are lies, and if we know they are lies we can stop Satan at his treacherous game. We can speak God's truth into situations in our lives. We can engage in the battle for the mind.

The Battleground of the Mind

Satan continually tries to sway and warp our way of thinking. Proverbs 23:7 says, "For as he thinks in his heart, so is he" (NKJV). We become what we think. This is why we spend a great deal of time in therapy teaching people how to think healthily. The enemy often uses the words that we have heard before against us. He whispers the messages of our soul wounds into our ears, making us feel hopeless. Even our very reactivity can be harnessed by Lucifer as a weapon formed against us. He sees our emotional overreaction and preys on our human weakness.

A father tells his son, "You're not good enough. You will never amount to anything." Satan reminds the son of these words with every failed attempt in his adult life, especially as a father. A dad does not see his daughter's talent and beauty. Satan is there to remind her that she is unworthy, particularly when her husband comes home late for the dinner she has labored over to entice him. When we feel inadequate about the awesome responsibility of parenting because we had poor role models, the enemy is there to remind us of our inadequacies again and again.

If we entertain the lies of the enemy we are actually tacitly agreeing with his messages about ourselves and our families. We are unwittingly forming an alliance with our mortal enemy. It is what we call an "Alliance of Lies." In this Alliance of Lies, Satan has but one purpose for us: to make sure that we believe the messages of our soul wounds and surrender to the enemy and subsequently to our own demise. Unfortunately, I'm very familiar with this game.

MORE OF BEV'S STORY

When I was a new Christian, Satan would repeat my mother's painful words in my ears. This reminder of my childhood pain and human inadequacies left me defenseless. I did not know how to fight him so I tacitly agreed with him, forming a spiritually deadly Alliance of Lies.

The lingering insidious murmurs of the enemy of my soul were intended to destroy me, and my unhealthy alliance with him was allowing this to continue in my life. Unfortunately, I entertained these painful, toxic thoughts regularly. After all, they were familiar. I was used to them. Remarks like "You're no good. . . . You're a stupid idiot who can't do anything right. . . . I wish you were never born" were like shards of glass in my chest. Satan would waste no time in reminding me of these statements, particularly when I was having a bad day, or had an important task ahead of me. When I spoke in front of our church youth group he would repeat my mother's painful words, "You're no good. You can't do that. You're a dumb, unwanted redneck girl. Why would anybody want to listen to you?"

Satan's barrage of lies followed me into my courtship with Tom. When we would have a disagreement, the sinister whispers of Lucifer were ever-present: *He doesn't love you. How could he if your own mother didn't love you?* The enemy's lies followed me into my early marriage, especially when we had a conflict. "Who do you think you are trying to do marriage? Your parents divorced and you will too." The lies haunted me acutely when I had children. "How would you know anything about raising children? Your mother bailed out on you and you're going to mess those girls up badly." These deceptions were killing me and I needed a way out.

I shared earlier that as a new Christian, I found solace in the book of Isaiah. Reading this helped me realize that I was not alone in my dilemma; the children of Judah were in the same situation.

THE WISDOM OF A SAGE

We read in the last chapter that the people of southern Israel made un-healthy alliances also. After losing their godly King Uzziah, Israel did not trust God's power or His promises for their future. No doubt the enemy was at work, even then, telling them the lie that God had aban-doned them. In their panic they turned to other sources for help and made unhealthy alliances with pagan nations. But God did not want His children trusting in man, He wanted them to trust in Him. So He gave Isaiah a prophecy for the destruction of those corrupt nations.

First Isaiah received an oracle that God would make the land desolate and destroy sinners within it (Isaiah 13:9). Then he received a prophecy about Babylon's demise in chapter 14. Babylon, now in modern-day Iraq, is still desolate in many ways to this day. Moab's downfall was next, then Damascus, in chapters 15–17, and there were many more to follow. Isaiah told God's people, "Turn to me and be saved, all you ends of the earth; for I am God, and there is no other. By myself I have sworn, my mouth has uttered in all integrity a word that will not be revoked: Before me every knee will bow; by me every tongue will swear. They will say of me, 'In the Lord alone are righteousness and strength'" (Isaiah 45:22–24).

What Isaiah is talking about here is a forsaking of our unhealthy, un-godly alliances. We need to turn to the Lord and be saved; saved from our thoughts, saved from ourselves, and saved from the lies of the enemy. As we bow to a holy God with our knees and confess with our tongues, God gives us the righteousness and strength to then renounce the un-healthy, ungodly alliances we have made.

SOLUTION

The solution to the Alliance of Lies that threatens to destroy us and our families is to *renounce*. To renounce means to repudiate or disown, to turn away from the unhealthy beliefs of the past. In fighting this battle for the mind, we have to take responsibility for our own destructive thoughts. Our lingering doubts and fears from past soul wounds can make very fertile ground for the enemy to plant his insidious seeds. We need to recognize how the enemy haunts us by repeating the messages of our soul wounds and infiltrating our minds with words of past pain, abuse, and failure. He lies to us and we can renounce these lies because they are not true.

It was great news for me to learn that the beliefs the enemy tried to instill in me were not true. They are not true for you either. These false-hoods were designed for our calamity but the Lord wants to bring us hope, and because of this, we can renounce our unhealthy, ungodly agreements and alliances and combat them with the soul-healing power of an unconditionally loving God. This realization has led us to Healing Premise #6.

HEALING PREMISE #6:

The enemy is a defeated foe in our lives, and applying
God's Word sets us free from his power.

It has been awesome for me to realize and experience that God is more powerful than the devil and that the enemy can be defeated in my life. As a new Christian I memorized 1 John 4:4: "Greater is he that is in you than he that is in the world" (KJV). And James 4:7: "Resist the devil, and he will flee from you" (KJV). I would recite them like a mantra when my mother would launch into an evil tirade about Christians or when my brother would bring his indigent addict friends to our house. Knowing that God was on my side helped me greatly to renounce the words of the enemy and quiet his lies.

While renouncing Lucifer's injurious fabrications, I found a small passage of Scripture that changed my life. By now, I am sure you are not surprised that it came from the wisdom of Isaiah. When you read these few words, read them like you are a frightened child, or like you depend on them for your dear life, because in so many ways, you do. "So do not fear, for I am with you" (Isaiah 41:10). These nine simple words set me free and subsequently became my mission statement. For someone who had lived in fear my whole life, these nine little words were transcendent. They meant that I belonged to someone and something. They meant that I could renounce my agreements with Satan and form new ones with a loving God who heals my soul.

We have developed several steps to renouncing the Alliance of Lies with the enemy. They involve asking yourself three questions. They are:

1. What are Lucifer's lies? (Often they will be echoes of the painful voices from childhood.)
2. Who or what taught you these messages?
3. In the light of God's Word, are they true?

You can ask yourself the last question and you, too, will receive the same answer from the Lord that I have always received. It is a resounding "No!" All you have to do is look at Scripture and you will see that you can renounce the lies of the enemy with God's Word.

Isaiah 41:9–13 says, "I took you from the ends of the earth, from its farthest corners I called you. I said, 'You are my servant'; I have chosen you and have not rejected you. So do not fear, for I am with you; do not be dismayed, for I am your God. I will strengthen you and help you; I will uphold you with my righteous right hand. All who rage against you will surely be ashamed and disgraced; those who oppose you will be as nothing and perish. Though you search for your enemies, you will not find them. Those who wage war against you will be as nothing at all. For I am the Lord, your God, who takes hold of your right hand and says to you, Do not fear; I will help you."

Wow, what awesome news! The war is over and the Lord has defeated our foe. All we have to do is trust in Him and claim our victory. There was a time in my life not too long ago when this Scripture passage and many others like it became like a spiritual armor for me when I battled with my fiendish adversary one more time.

Chapter Twelve

Doing Battle with the Enemy

*O*ne spring day I received a call that my mother had died suddenly of an aneurysm. No one was with her because she had alienated all of her children and family members. She died alone. Frankly, I was not surprised, but as her daughter this grieved my spirit greatly. A year went by and we all knew that we had to go back into that horrible house we once called home in order to clean it and prepare it to be sold. It was either this or have the city condemn it and I just could not do that to the neighbors.

As you can imagine, none of us children, including me, wanted to step one foot back in that house where we experienced so much evil. The memories of that home were frightening and painful. While I lived there I often felt the forces of darkness surround me. Frequently, I looked into my mother's eyes and saw evil. This was horrifying for a child. The thought of going back there created cold chills down my spine. When it came time to go, none of my siblings could go with me. Can you blame them? So Tom and I set out on this precarious journey together.

A foreboding feeling filled my chest on the four-hour drive to my pitiful childhood home. Tom and I listened to praise music and worshipped the entire way. I had memorized a passage from Isaiah in preparation for the trip. These words were like a balm to my wounded soul as I prepared. "I, even I, am he who comforts you. Who are you that you fear mortal men, the sons of men, who are but grass" (Isaiah 51:12).

This passage helped me realize that since I had the power of the Lord with me, I had no need to fear mortal man, not even the memory of mortal man—or woman. Isaiah 51:13b says, [Who are you] "that you live in constant terror every day because of the wrath of the oppressor?" Every time I read this passage, I thought that God was reading my mail! Terror was my constant companion in that house. The passage goes on to say, "The cowering prisoners will be set free; they will not die in their dungeon" (Isaiah 51:14a). This passage was particularly meaningful because there were times in that house that I feared for my life. I was sure that I was going to die in that dingy dungeon. But this promise gave me hope in the midst of my terror.

When we arrived at my childhood home, I vividly remember getting out of the car and walking to the front porch with fear and trepidation, only to find that when I entered, my enemies were nowhere to be found and those who waged war against me were as nothing at all (Isaiah 41:12). I walked through the tiny, dark, and dirty rooms where pain, suffering, and abuse had once occurred, and I felt God's presence. I felt Him take me by his "righteous right hand" (Isaiah 41:10b) and lead me from room to painful room. In each one I renounced my Alliance of Lies with the enemy, and all the while the Lord was whispering His loving truths to me. *You have nothing to be afraid of. I am here with you. I have redeemed you from the evil you suffered here as a child. You are Mine,* echoed in my ears and penetrated my soul.

As I walked through the rooms of that awful house that held so many hideous memories for me, I truly felt the supernatural power of the Lord envelop me as He spoke a peace that quelled my fear. "You did it, Father." I whispered, in worship to Him. "You saved the dumb unwanted redneck girl from all of this hell. You did it. Thank you, Abba. Thank you forever, Daddy."

During that time and many others, I have needed divine help to do battle with Satan. Unfortunately, if you have had family members who ushered in evil, you, too, will need to frequently call on this divine help just as I did. The amazing thing to me is that after all these years, He is always there. Much to my dismay, I could never count on my parents to be there for me, but I can always count on the Lord. For this child of abuse, this assurance is mind-blowing.

There are so many times that I have wondered why the Lord allowed the enemy to taunt me so frequently—and through someone who was supposed to love and nurture me, no less. After years of serving the Lord, I now know it is because the Lord was using everything that happened to me to teach me His ways. He was preparing me even then for the call He had on my life and the goodness He had in store for me. We must stay vigilant to Satan's tactics, but we need not worry about his power. We have a power much greater to combat his lies.

ASK THE LORD TO PARENT YOU

In the last chapter we talked about renouncing the Alliance of Lies. After you do this, you begin to fill your mind with the voice of the Lord. He tells you the truth about yourself—that you are His and He will not abandon you. He becomes like a parent to you. If you are like me, He becomes the parents you never had—and it's amazing.

I was in college when I finally figured out that I was an emotional orphan. I had parents that provided some basic care for me but they were not there spiritually, emotionally, and psychologically to nurture my heart, mind, and soul. Not having parents was hard for me. You may know what I'm talking about. My mother's unpredictable outbursts caused me to feel like I was walking on broken glass most of my childhood. She was not there at times when I really needed a mother. My father left our family when I was small and I saw him infrequently for a few hours, but it just was not enough. I would see kids at church with their parents and wish so badly that I had parents who would do things

with me, go to church with me, instruct me, and pray with me. I decided
to ask the Lord to mother and father me. I now tell all of my clients to
do this, particularly those who grew up in homes like mine. It may be
good for you, too.

Maybe your parents were not physically or emotionally abusive, but
they were simply not there. Dad was gone chasing the American dream
and Mom was preoccupied or shut down. Perhaps your parents were
missionaries and felt like they had to put a lot of energy into the na-
tionals, leaving you to feel neglected and alone. Possibly your parents
were wonderful but they have gone to be with the Lord, and you feel
abandoned. Whatever the situation, ask the Lord to be your mother and
your father.

A New Mother and Father

After praying for the Lord to parent me, I began to feel like the Lord was
my father. He provided masculine energy in my soul that guided me,
protected me, made me feel safe, and affirmed. That's what daddies do.
They "contend with those who contend with you" (Isaiah 49:25b). They
watch your back!

I then saw that the Holy Spirit was my mother. This *paraclete* em-
bodies God's feminine characteristics as it nurtures me, walks beside me,
and takes care of me like a mother would. Isaiah 49:15a says, "Can a
woman forget her nursing child, And not have compassion on the son
of her womb?" (NKJV). Once again, concerning my earthly mother, my
answer would be either "Yes" or "It depends on what mood she's in." But
I have learned to take comfort in Isaiah's words, which say, "Surely they
may forget, Yet I will not forget you" (vs. 15b, NKJV). Time and time
again, the Holy Spirit has not forgotten me.

When I think of all the things that my loving heavenly parents have protected me from, I am stricken with gratitude and moved to tears. Someone else in my situation might have become mentally ill, addicted to drugs, had a series of trashed relationships, or abused her own children. But the soul-healing love of the Lord rescued me and parented me and still does to this day.

My childhood was nothing like I would have wanted. Many nights I cried myself to sleep, wishing I could be anywhere but there. My sister would do the same and we would often take turns patting each other in empathy as we drifted off to sleep—a fitting escape from the pain. But we were only to wake up the next day and realize that things had not changed. We were still in sheol! But even during all of that, the Lord was there for me.

This Easter, I celebrated 40 years of serving the Lord. For four wonderful decades, He has fought with my oppressor, guided me, and protected my children from the wiles of the enemy (and the ignorance of their parents). I wanted my childhood to be different. I wanted my parents to be different. I wanted my circumstances to be different. But the Lord did not give me what I wanted. It took some time for me to see that He gave me what I needed. And He was there every step of the way while I journeyed. I ran across a wonderful poem that says this so much better than I can. The author was an unknown Confederate soldier, but I hope he will see in heaven the comfort these verses have brought to so many, including me.

I Asked God for Strength
I asked God for strength that I might achieve,
I was made weak that I might learn humbly to obey.
I asked for health that I might do greater things,
I was given infirmity that I might do better things.
I asked for riches that I might be happy,

I was given poverty that I might be wise.
I asked for power that I might have the praise of men,
I was given weakness that I might feel the need of God.
I asked for all things that I might enjoy life,
I was given life that I might enjoy all things.
I got nothing that I asked for, but everything that I hoped for,
Almost despite myself, my unspoken prayers were answered.
I am, among all men, most richly blessed!

THE SMITHS DO BATTLE WITH THE ENEMY

Bill, Amy, Chloe, and Billy Smith entered our office and took their usual places as Amy collected all of the jackets and placed them neatly over a wing chair before she sat down. Billy kept his book bag in front of him because he was eager to show us his Star Wars action figures.

"Are we still gonna talk about war today?" he asked eagerly. "'Cause I have some of my warriors to show you. I use them to play interplanetary war." His entire shoulder was inside the book bag as he searched for every action figure he could find. He then pulled them all out and placed them in front of us.

"Wow, they are amazing," Tom said. "They look real and their arms and legs move," Tom continued, as he took a two-inch plastic light saber and put it in Anakin Skywalker's hand. He, Chloe, and Billy proceeded to have a mini sword battle, complete with sound effects, while their parents and I cheered them on.

After a few minutes, Tom said, "The battle is over and the good guys won. Let's put our warriors back in the book bag and talk about the real war that is going on in our lives." As the kids put their toys away, Tom asked the family how they did on their homework.

Amy spoke up, "Bill was gone for four days on a fishing trip."

"Yeah, and I wanted to go but Daddy said it was just for grown-ups and guys," Chloe chimed in.

"I said that I would take you sometime by yourself," Bill defended himself.

"That's a great idea," Tom praised.

"Can we go this weekend?" Chloe questioned impulsively.

"Not this weekend but sometime," her dad responded.

Amy broke in, trying to get the family back on track. "Before Bill left, we started the Four R's for our family devotions. We did the first two and it has been great."

Bill added, "I read the Isaiah passages over and over while I was away on my trip and I think they have really helped me. Since you told us more about spiritual warfare, I have been paying more attention to the voices in my head."

"Yeah, me too," Billy added. "I've felt like Satan was telling me this week that Chloe was unfair and that I should hit her. But I remembered what you said, Dr. Bev, and I talked to her instead."

"Great job, Buddy!" Bill said, and Billy soaked up the praise like a sponge.

Bill then said, "I have never really thought much about Satan until our last meeting. I just thought of him as something the nuns used to use to scare us kids in parochial school; that, and beating us on the knuckles with a ruler!" Everyone in the room laughed.

"What do you think of the enemy of our souls now, Bill?" Tom asked.

"I think that for years I have believed the lies of my childhood which made it easy for him to taunt me with them. I want that to stop. I am tired of Satan reminding me of my past and stealing my and my family's happiness."

"Bill, you are talking like a true warrior," Tom commended, "by saying that you are ready to do battle and protect yourself and your family. That's what warriors do. That's what fathers do."

"Yeah, Dad, you're like Luke Skywalker," Billy chirped, adding battle noises.

We then shared the same concepts with them that we shared with you—concepts like the Alliance of Lies, renouncing, asking the Lord to mother and father you, and Healing Premise #6.

Next we taught them an exercise called The Truster Reconstructor which was developed by my sister, Linda Newton, who is a pastoral counselor in Northern California. She details this exercise in her book *Twelve Ways to Turn Your Pain Into Praise.* In that book she shares more stories of our childhood pain and how the Lord helped us trade beauty for ashes and praise for despair. The Truster Reconstructor was a key exercise in doing that. She uses other passages of Scripture but we found the book of Isaiah to be particularly meaningful. In following Linda's example we listed key passages from the wise scribe and left blank spaces for people to write their names and appropriate personal pronouns. This would make the scriptures personal.

We handed the Truster Reconstructor to each member of the Smith family, and Amy and Chloe were asked to help Billy if he needed it. They were then told to make copies and put them up in key places where they would see them often. They could put them on the refrigerator, the computer screen, the dashboard of the car, and anywhere else where they would read them daily.

"That's a great idea," Amy said. "I have a laminator and I can laminate them so that they will last."

"I'm going to put mine on my lunch box, and on my mirror in my room," Chloe said excitedly.

"I'm gonna put mine on my Star Wars toy box," Billy replied.

"Sounds like you guys are getting the idea of this exercise. You'll have to let us know all the places you put them when you come back to see us. But remember, you have to read it every time you see it or it won't help," I instructed.

"Do we get a prize for how many times we read it?" Chloe asked.

"The prize will be how well your soul feels," I said as I looked at Bill and Amy and smiled. "But I think that Dr. Tom and I can come up with something for you before you come back!" We then scheduled a time for them to return, knowing that these scriptures would help them tremendously.

What about you? Has this chapter made you more aware of the war you are engaged in? If so, here is some Healing Homework to help you.

HEALING HOMEWORK

- ~ Write a prayer renouncing the Alliance of Lies you have made with the enemy as he has haunted you with your past. Have each family member do the same.
- ~ Pray these prayers as a family and share the answers to your prayers regularly.
- ~ Complete the Truster Reconstructor from Isaiah on the next page, filling in the blanks with your name and the proper personal pronouns in the blank spaces.
- ~ Make copies of this sheet and put it where you will see it and read it daily as a reminder of God's unconditional soul-healing love.
- ~ Read the sheets aloud at family devotions, meetings, or dinner.
- ~ Have each family member find other passages of Scripture and personalize them as well.
- ~ Discuss with your spouse and children what the words of these passages mean to you.

TRUSTER RECONSTRUCTOR (ISAIAH)

Isaiah 30:15b In quietness and trust is _____'s strength.
Isaiah 30:18–21 Yet the Lord longs to be gracious to _____;
he rises to show _____ compassion. For the Lord is a God
of justice. Blessed are all who wait for Him! _____ will weep no more.
How gracious [God] will be when _____ cries for help! As
soon as he hears he will answer _____. Although the Lord
gives _____ the bread of adversity and the water of affliction … Whether _____ turns to the right or to the left,
_____'s ears will hear [His] voice behind _____,
saying, This is the way; walk in it. **Isaiah 43:10b** _____ is
my servant whom I have chosen, so that _____ may know
and believe me and understand that I am he. **Isaiah 45:2–5** I [the Lord]
will go before _____ and will level the mountains; I
will break down gates of bronze and cut through bars of iron. I will give
_____ the treasures of darkness, riches stored in secret
places, so that _____ may know that I am the Lord, the
God of Israel, who summons _____ by name … [I] bestow
on _____ a title of honor … I am the Lord … and apart
from me there is no [other] God. I will strengthen _____.
Isaiah 49:1b Before _____ was born I [God] called
_____; from _____'s birth he has made mention
of _____'s name. **Isaiah 53:5** But he was pierced for
_____'s transgressions, he was crushed for _____'s
iniquities; the punishment that brought _____ peace was
upon him, and by his wounds _____ is healed.

Chapter Thirteen

Identifying and Understanding Your Needs

om and I came out into the waiting room to the sound of laughter. Chloe's petite frame was enveloped by Bill's arms as she sat on his lap playing a tickle game. Billy was strategically perched on the floor by Dad's feet trying to get a good tickle in while Dad was preoccupied with his sister. Amy tried to read snippets of a *Highlights* magazine in between giggles, as she smiled with delight. Bill was laughing in a way that we had never seen before. His expression of joy captivated us, and no one wanted it to end. We waited a while, basking in the bliss, before we asked them to come into the inner office.

As they started into our office, Amy asked if she and Bill could come in alone for the first half of the session.

"Uh-oh, when she does this, I'm usually in trouble," Bill remarked.

"No, you're not in trouble," Amy said, getting crayons and coloring books out for Billy and Chloe. She spread the crayons and paper out in front of them and reminded them to be quiet for the next half hour. They gladly busied themselves as their parents entered our office. "No fighting," Amy added, opening the inner door to our office. The children barely looked up, already engrossed in their artwork.

"We are doing so much better," said Amy as she made herself

comfortable on the sofa close to Bill. "You guys have taught us so much. We have learned to appreciate the areas where we are opposites. We use the GIFT exercise as a family and it makes things run much more smoothly. Our prayer and devotional life has changed drastically. What I wanted to discuss, though, is how we can keep from getting stuck on each other's soul wounds." Amy shifted the pillow in her lap to get more comfortable. Leaning forward, she continued.

"I almost feel guilty saying this because things are going so well. You saw us out there," she said, as she gestured toward the waiting room door. "I don't want Bill to think that I'm being critical or hard to please. I think that we have done great work as a family, but it's just that I want our family to keep growing." Amy heaved a sigh of relief, then looked at Bill for some reassuring feedback.

Bill's response amazed her. "I agree," he said with a twinkle in his eye, obviously knowing that she would be pleased. "I want to keep growing too. I think we have changed a lot, but I can see that we still get stuck as a family. Just the other day Amy got on me for coming home late from work. The kids joined her and they all started riding me, and I'm afraid that I got defensive and said some things. I didn't get as mad as I used to." He then looked at Tom and me and winked, "See, I have learned something in all of these months. But all of us were upset with each other and didn't know what to do."

"What did you do?" I asked.

"We all sat in tense silence through most of dinner," Amy interjected.

"That is much better than fighting like we used to do," Bill defended.

"But it is still uncomfortable and we would love to learn a better way to handle this," Amy replied. "We were at a loss and wondered what we were supposed to do. I thought we could ask you guys how to get out of these ditches."

Tom and I looked at each other and gave a nod that we were thinking the same thing and Tom said, "Bev and I think you are ready to learn another communication technique in the Soul-Healing Love Model, one that will help you go deeper in dealing with each other's soul wounds. The tool is aptly named the Digging Deeper exercise. But, before we do this, we want to teach you a few things about communication. Are you guys game?" Both Bill and Amy were nodding enthusiastically, so we proceeded to teach them the information we are about to teach you. The first part has to do with basic needs.

CRITICISM VERSUS NEEDS

Research shows that most couples introduce thorny issues in the family with a complaint or criticism. This is an unhealthy practice and it predicts divorce in couples.[1] A better way to introduce conflict in the family is to make a statement about how you feel and what you need rather than simply being critical. Besides, most people get defensive when criticized so it isn't very beneficial to start a conflict in this manner. So, instead of saying, "You don't care enough about the family to come home on time," you could say, "We miss you when you don't get home earlier." This is a softer, more positive way to state what is troubling you.

We also know that behind every complaint or criticism is a *need*. If you say that you miss spending time with your mate, your need is *connection*. You want your mate to spend more time with you so that you can get that need met. If I complain to Tom that he doesn't help me enough with the chores, my need is *support*. I want to feel that he is with me and I'm not doing everything all by myself. Tom's help with the chores can actually make me feel special to him, thus meeting my need for *significance*. Interestingly, help with chores does not necessarily show Tom that he is special to me or give him a sense of significance. His need for significance is met in different ways. So you see, what meets a need for one mate may not meet it for another.

When family members introduce conflicts and disappointments

with criticism, their real needs get lost in the rhetoric. This is called a critical start-up, and when it happens, it is easy for families to get defensive, which further obscures each person's true needs. Too often families do not share their needs, they just complain and criticize. We believe that one of the main reasons for this problem is because many people do not know what they need.

It's true. Many people walk around in relationships every day unaware of their true needs. This means that if they are disappointed or upset with their spouse or children, they will have no idea how to get out of their power struggle because they do not know what they need. It stands to reason that if you don't know what you need, there is little likelihood that that need will get met. This is a formula for misunderstanding, disappointment, and pain. Yet we see it every day with families.

Humans are not born needless. Infants scream at 2:00 A.M. when they are hungry. They coo, preen, and laugh on cue for attention. We were all born knowing what we needed and we were not hesitant to ask. But somewhere along the way, many of us learned that having needs was not a good thing. If you lived in a family that did not care about your needs, shamed you for having needs, or simply did not meet them, then you may have learned to repress these needs well below your conscious mind. This can make it hard to know what you need in relationships.

KNOWING WHAT YOU NEED

I (Bev) had a hard time knowing what I needed in relationships. Perhaps it was because my needs were rarely met. Being a single mom with four kids was too much for my mom. She worked at night as a waitress/bartender and slept all day to escape her misery. On the occasions that she was awake, she would stand at the screen door of our disheveled house and bark orders at us.

"Get the clothes off the line, tend to your baby brother, get in here and fix some food for you kids to eat," she would shriek. At age nine, I was a little adult. In family therapy, we call this a "parentified child." The problem with being a parentified child is that you don't have time to get your childhood needs met. Children need to play, have sleepovers, and go to birthday parties. But most of my childhood was spent working and caring for others.

When I would ask to do the things that normal kids did, that is, get my childhood needs met, my mom would bellow, "Why would I allow you to have a sleepover? I don't need any more kids around here driving me crazy. Playing is silly and frivolous. Besides, you have too much work to do to play." It's no wonder that I became a workaholic and spent years recovering. But my mom's most famous line when we asked for something was, "So you want that; well, people in jail want out and you don't see them getting out do you? If they don't get what they want, what makes you think that you can?" I'm serious; she really said that. When I speak across the globe and share this story, most people look at me with incredulity and sadness in their eyes.

"Mom, can I go to Susan's house to play?" I would plead. "People in jail want out."

"Mom, can I to go to the church picnic?" "People in jail want out." And so our conversations went, throughout my childhood. I often felt like those prisoners she referenced, wanting out of my confinement. If I ever bucked her, and it was rare, I would get slapped or switched until the welts drew blood. But, this did not sting nearly as much as the words she said as she swung. "You are so selfish and think only of what you want," she would say. "There are four people in this house and all you can think about is yourself." I heard these statements so often that I started to believe them. They became tattooed to my soul. By age nine, I thought that having needs was selfish and I banished them from my conscious mind. I became needless. My whole existence came to be about meeting everyone else's needs. This is a formula for severe codependency, and I was a supreme candidate.

Not surprisingly, after I married Tom and he and I would fight, I would try to tell him what I needed, but the words would not come. Since I didn't know what I needed, I had trouble getting needs met. When this happened, I typically assumed the worst about Tom. *Tom is like everyone else. He doesn't care about my needs either,* I thought. This negative assumption haunted me until I learned how to get in touch with my needs.

We shared earlier that Tom grew up in a home where there was a great deal of tension between his parents. They subsequently divorced when he was grown, but the tension took its toll on him. His father and mother were estranged a good bit of the time, which caused his mother to turn to him for solace and companionship. This was hard because at an early age, he felt like he had to be responsible for her happiness. She was unhappy in her marriage to Tom's dad, so he felt the burden to make things better. In caretaking his mother, he would feel guilty if he wanted to go play with his friends and leave her alone. He often felt bad asking to get his own needs met. So he learned early to repress them by pushing them out of his conscious mind. He, too, introduced conflict by criticizing and blaming. Like me, he did not know what he needed to resolve the conflict. We got stuck so many times in our early marriage that we set out on a course to determine what our needs actually were. We found that the best way to do this is to look at basic needs.

BASIC NEEDS

Tom and I decided to make a list of the things humans need to feel healthy and whole. If these needs are not met, soul wounds can occur. These needs are:

- **Love**—to be unconditionally accepted for who you are.
- **Security**—to know that you will not by harmed or abandoned.
- **Safety**—there will be no tissue damage, property damage, or soul damage.
- **Nurturance**—you will have food, shelter, and clothing, and be hugged and touched appropriately and often.
- **Understanding**—you can be who you are, understood for who you are, and loved for who you are.
- **Affirmation**—to have your gifts and abilities recognized.
- **Connection**—to belong and be a part of something that is greater than yourself.
- **Support**—to have someone to help sustain you and hold you up, to have guidance and advice in life.
- **Significance**—to feel special and important to someone and know that your needs and desires matter.

Now, we know that there are many more needs to be met in people such as challenge and creativity, but this list shows the deeper needs—the soul needs. These are the needs that are most likely to result in soul wounds if they are not met. Humans do not get these soul needs met when abandonment, abuse, and neglect occur. Some parents neglect these needs as an act of omission. The work-addicted father or the stoic mother may not intend to wound their children, but they do so by default. Some parents neglect the needs of their children by commission. The punitive, abusive, alcoholic father and the angry, sadistic mother are examples of this. Whatever the case, knowing what you need will greatly increase the likelihood of your getting those needs met now and resolving family conflict in a healthier way.

One more reason people have learned to repress their needs is the fear that they will not get them met. Many people fear that they are being weak if they need something from someone. They believe that needlessness is noble or healthy. Because of this they do not want to be vulnerable enough to actually state what they need. Vulnerability can be scary, especially with those you love. *What if I ask for what I need and you do not care enough to give it to me?* you may think of those closest to you. If you think this way, you are not alone. Unfortunately, it is a universal problem. It is human nature to resist meeting others' needs as they resist yours. It's no wonder we fear being vulnerable enough to state our needs! This is such a common problem that there's a statement about it in the Soul-Healing Love model: "Requirement equals resistance."

REQUIREMENT EQUALS RESISTANCE

It is human nature that people tend to resist if you require something from them. People prefer choice rather than obligation. Requirement is seen as a form of constraint rather than an option. This concept is also taught in sales seminars. Sales people are encouraged to offer their customers choices so they have a better chance of getting a sale. Another common example is toddlers in a nursery. A two-year-old can pick up a toy and become easily disenchanted with it. He may quickly put it down and busily move to something else. But, if another toddler picks it up (requires it), you will see that first toddler scream with resistance. His original toy becomes his prized possession because someone else requires it.

Unfortunately, this notion plagues adults too. Let's say that every day your neighbor, Ellie May, comes home before you do and brings your paper from the curb to your front porch. She does this by choice. *What a nice gesture*, you think. Then one day, you go over to Ellie May's house and say, "Hey, Ellie, can you bring my paper in earlier today? I have the afternoon off and I want to read it." Do you think that your good neighbor, Ellie, will ever bring in your paper again? Probably not! You took her choice away by requiring something and you can bet she will resist.

Families are just as guilty of this as toddlers in a nursery or hospitable neighbors. They can have every excuse in the world not to meet each other's needs. Some may even be legitimate, but resistance is usually lying underneath. This is sad, but it is the human condition. Human beings are born sinful, and we tend to be selfish. The tendency to be selfish goes against the grain of what the Lord wants us to be, particularly in families. He wants us to be sacrificial and unconditionally loving. Unfortunately this can be hard to do.

RESISTANCE IN THE FAMILY

It is sad that we resist those closest to us. You would think that we would want to do more for family, but the old adage, "Familiarity breeds contempt," can apply here. Let's face it: family relationships are based on requirement. We have much higher expectations of family than of anyone else on the planet, so it stands to reason that we can resist them on an unconscious or even conscious level. Also, we can't forget that Satan is at work, telling us that we are being asked to do too much, give too much, or be too sacrificial for our loved ones. He whispers to us that the situation is unfair, that we are doing far more than our spouses, children, or siblings. And because of that we should resist to even the score or teach them a lesson. This line of thinking causes the family to become a veritable breeding ground for resistance, causing pain. It is just not biblical. First John 4:7 says, "Dear friends, let us love one another, for love comes from God. Everyone who loves has been born of God and knows God."

Sadly, it is much easier to do things for our neighbors, our classmates, or even our work colleagues, than for our families. We hear people say this all the time. "I just wish she treated me like she treats the neighbor." Or "I want him to treat me the way he treats the people on the church board." The reverse is also true when people say, "Everybody on the church board loves me" or "My secretary treats me better than my wife does."

What we typically say to those people is, "Perhaps they would not love you so freely if you started requiring them to." If there was constraint, they might just resist. If they lived with you day in and day out, if they had the capacity to hurt you like family, then you might not feel their love and appreciation as much as you do now that they have the choice.

If a colleague at work did not want to eat dinner with you, you might feel a little slighted, but if your children refused, you would feel hurt. Closeness can breed hurt, and when we are hurt, we tend to withhold love. It is true that no one can trigger us like family, and no one can hurt us like family. But, the opposite is also true: *No one can heal us like family either.*

So, how do we motivate family members to stop this selfish, childish behavior? How do we get them to move toward each other and overcome the resistance that requirement elicits? That's what we'll be talking about in the next chapter.

Chapter Fourteen

Making Healing Practical: Communication Tools That Bring About Understanding and Empathy

*N*ow that you have identified your needs and you understand that requirement equals resistance, what do you do with this information? How do the members of your family all learn to care for one another in a healing way? The answer is found in God's great *agape* love.

AGAPE

There is no better place to look for help in teaching families how to care for each other than the Author of agape—the God of the universe who sacrificed His Son that we might live eternally (John 3:16). God the Father loves us unconditionally. Nothing we can do will ever separate us from that love (Romans 5:8). That's agape love. As we bathe in the unconditional love of Christ who died for us, how can we not want to allow that love to spill out over our family? Because Christ agaped us, we can have agape for our family. In growing this agape, it is important to allow each family member to share their innermost feelings and to listen to what each one is trying to say. We call this *listening with agape*. In order to learn more about how to do this, we are once again going to look at the book of Isaiah.

The Wisdom of a Sage

Often in Scripture we see that agricultural or farming metaphors illustrate the spiritual life. Isaiah was no exception to this rule. As he tried to tell the people of Judah about God's impending judgment for their idolatry, he compared their spiritual lives to dry twigs (Isaiah 27:11). Trees in the Bible often represent spiritual life. The people of Israel were likened to rotten branches that could waver and blow in the wind. Planting often represents one's connection and service to others, and threshing is a metaphor for God's purging. The Lord prunes and purges us to make us better equipped for faithful service.

Isaiah 28:23–29 says, "Listen and hear my voice; pay attention and hear what I say. When a farmer plows for planting, does he plow continually? Does he keep on breaking up and harrowing the soil? When he has leveled the surface, does he not sow caraway and scatter cummin? Does he not plant wheat in its place, barley in its plot, and spelt in its field? His God instructs him and teaches him the right way. Caraway is not threshed with a sledge, nor is a cartwheel rolled over cummin; caraway is beaten out with a rod, and cummin with a stick. Grain must be ground to make bread; so one does not go on threshing it forever. . . . All this also comes from the Lord Almighty, wonderful in counsel and magnificent in wisdom."

When I read this passage I am amazed at how specific the Lord is about the planting of each special plant and herb. Because they are tender and young, the farmer is instructed to use special tools. In this passage you can see that the Lord specifically instructs the farmer to take into account how fragile they are. In the same way, the Lord takes in all of our weaknesses and special circumstances when He grows us. He deals with each of us individually with sensitivity. This is a great pattern for how we should deal with our family members, especially the young tender children. In listening to our family members with agape, we have to respond with the appropriate tools. We can't scatter our loved ones on the rocky soil of control or fear. We can't use criticism and negativity as a threshing tool. Self-esteem is harvested with praise and encouragement. Each family relationship is a tender herb that needs special attention and the Lord Almighty who is "wonderful in counsel and magnificent in wisdom" can teach us how to do this (Isaiah 28:29). It is our job to listen to Him.

INEFFECTIVE TOOLS

In the past three decades, we have worked with thousands of families. In doing so, we have seen several common mistakes they make while trying to listen with agape. Learning to stop these unhealthy behaviors can produce healthy, hearty plants. We will share some of them with you so you can help your garden to grow gracefully.

1. Trying to listen while distracted.

Women are more guilty of this than men; perhaps it is because they are multitaskers. Men, however, fall prey to this while watching TV or reading the newspaper. Both genders need to be intentional listeners, especially with their children.

When our daughters were still living at home, one of them would come home from school with something on her heart that she needed to share. It could have been about friends, her spiritual life, or a dating relationship. I am ashamed to say that although I make a living reading people's moods and getting them to open up, I would miss a perfectly good opportunity with my own children. Like most moms, I was stirring spaghetti, making airline reservations on the phone, petting the dog with my foot, and calling out spelling words. All at the same time! I had to learn to tune in to what my child was saying and stop the "tyranny of the urgent" long enough to hear her heart. That was not an easy task for a busy beaver like me, but it was essential in learning to listen with agape.

2. Interrogating versus asking good questions.

It is important that family members ask questions without sounding like they are interviewing a witness in a courtroom. This is particularly hard for parents of teenagers. Teens don't like to feel like they are being grilled. "Where did you go?" "Who were you with?" "What time did you get home?" "Were your friend's parents there?" are all good questions. But, if they are asked in a harsh, untrusting style you can be sure your teen (and other family members) will resist answering you.

Several years ago I worked with a family that had a 15-year-old daughter named Hannah who was making failing grades, skipping class, constantly sassing her parents, and hanging out with some unsavory friends. Her mom told me that she had stopped sharing what was going on in her life and spent most days in her room with her iPod earphones growing out of her ears, or texting her friends on her cell phone. Her parents tried grounding her and restricting her from using her various electronic devices for her rebellious behavior, but none of these seemed to work. In fact, the punishments were driving their family further apart.

My goal as their family counselor was to get Mom, Dad, and daughter connecting and communicating again. It did not take long to see what was breaking down in this family's communication style. Mom and Dad both pleaded, cajoled, and finally ranted at Hannah to open up to them.

"Stop shutting us out," they would beg. "We have a right to know what is going on in your life. We can handle what you tell us." I took them up on their offer and encouraged Hannah to confide in her parents. She told them that her best friend, Bethany, had tried alcohol. Her parents hit the roof, became hysterical, and forbade her to see Bethany again. They were outraged that they had trusted Bethany and allowed Hannah to sleep over at her house numerous times, saying that Bethany had conned and betrayed them. It took months for me to get this family back on track after this near-fatal communication mistake. As hard as it is, we need to stay calm, even when we hear alarming news from our children. After all, we want them to continue to share.

3. Having Unhealthy Expectations

One of the most harmful things you can do is to have unhealthy expectations of family members. These can negatively affect spouses, but they can be particularly deadly in dealing with children. Here are a few that can be most harmful.

- Expecting your children to be little adults and perform both emotional and physical tasks that are beyond their years, such as taking care of you or giving them chores beyond their physical capabilities.
- Expecting your child to be just like you or do things only the way you do them. There is more than one way to bake a cake. Perhaps the Lord gave you your children to grow you and help you see things from another perspective.
- Living through your child. Putting all of your unmet childhood needs on your child can be very unhealthy. If you did not get to take piano lessons or play Little League ball, you may be determined to have your children do these things. The problem is that they may not be interested. Dragging your resistant child to music lessons or being an over-involved sideline coach can harm them.

EMPATHY

Avoiding all of these unhealthy expectations can help you listen to your child with agape, and thus use the right harvesting tools on the fragile, tender herbs we call children. There is a single thread that winds around all of these unhealthy communication patterns: the lack of empathy. One of the surest ways your family can learn to listen to each other and meet requirements without innate resistance is to put yourselves in each other's shoes. In other words, have empathy for each other. This brings us to our final healing premise.

> HEALING PREMISE #7:
> *Put yourself in the other's shoes. Empathy is the key that unlocks love in families.*

Empathy is the identification with or the vicarious experiencing of the feelings and thoughts of another. Empathy is the key ingredient that allows the Holy Spirit to fill us with agape. It is much harder to resist someone's requirement when you have empathy. In the Soul-Healing Love Model we have developed a tool to help families dig deeper than their requirements, move further than their own needs, and develop empathy for themselves and empathy for others. It helps them put themselves in each other's shoes and become aware of each other's soul wounds so that they can feel for other family members. This enables them to better meet their own and each other's needs. We call this tool the Digging Deeper exercise.

THE DIGGING DEEPER EXERCISE

This exercise is a continuance or spin-off of the GIFT exercise in chapter 4. We first developed the Digging Deeper exercise for couples, but it was not long before parents were trying it with their children and other family members and found it to be quite successful. The exercise consists of five questions and starts with the typical family complaint or criticism. We call this a trigger. The first question is about that trigger.

Question #1: What do you do that triggers me?
You will need to introduce the trigger calmly and without verbal or non-verbal accusation. Therapist and researcher John Gottman found that one of the predictors of divorce for couples is a "hard start-up" when conflict is introduced.[1] Dr. Gottman's findings are echoed in the book of Proverbs, which says, "A soft answer turns away wrath, but harsh words cause quarrels" (Proverbs 15:1, TLB). So, when you bring up a trigger, instead of doing it in the form of a criticism or complaint, do it softly using this format: "When you . . . I feel . . ." This stops the blame game or critical "you" statements, which make a person feel blamed or criticized.

In the early years of our marriage, when Tom was a pastor, one of my big triggers was when he would get wrapped up in his work and forget to call to let me know when he was coming home. I would usually get upset and attack him saying, "You are so inconsiderate not to stop by a pay phone and call me to let me know you're okay." (There were no cell phones in those days.) This is a hard start-up and would guarantee that Tom would return my anger with more anger. To begin this trigger with a soft start-up, I learned to say, "When you're late and don't call, I feel . . ." Now I needed to know what I felt. This is where the GIFT exercise comes in. Use the GIFT exercise to determine the primary emotion that you feel.

Question #2: What do I feel about the trigger? Guilt, inferiority, fear, or trauma (hurt)?
In our marital dilemma, I felt both fear and inferiority: fear that something had happened to Tom, and inferiority that I was not important enough for him to call me.

13

Next in the Digging Deeper exercise, you will want to determine if your feelings and emotions are tied to a soul wound. If you have reactivity, it is a sure bet that they are. Prayerfully ask yourself the following question.

Question #3: When have I felt this before?

Here is where real empathy is allowed to take root. We ask adults to look at their childhoods to determine where these feelings come from. We learned earlier that childhood wounds are the most potent because of old brain reactivity. So adults ask the Lord to show them what might be triggering such great emotion in them.

We ask children to look at situations in their lives when they felt deep emotion. These can cause reactivity now and later in their lives if not addressed. It can be hard for children because they have a limited number of memories, but we are continually surprised at how many children remember great details about their pasts. Some of the more traumatic memories in both children and adults may be repressed. The psyche has a way of helping us submerge extremely traumatic events deep into the recesses of our memory. If this is the case, prayerfully ask the Lord to help you retrieve that which He desires to heal. Remember the Holy Spirit is a gentleman and will only give you what you can handle at one time. It may take a while for memories to surface but God is faithful to heal them if we ask Him.

In asking myself question #3 of the Digging Deeper exercise, I discovered that Tom's coming home late without calling reminded me of the many painful times when my mother would leave us children alone until the wee hours of the morning. I would lie awake at night and worry about our safety. This caused me a great deal of anxiety and it took years for me to recover. When Tom would be late, he would pick the scab off of that soul wound and I would become reactive, which brings us to Question #4.

Question #4: What do I do when I feel this feeling?

Ask yourself what you do when you are upset about the trigger. Do you become reactive, get angry and yell, become passive-aggressive, or maybe even withdraw and pout in icy silence?

As a child, I wanted to confront my mother for her thoughtless behavior. I wanted to get angry and let her have it. But my mother would never have tolerated that. I learned early in life that you could never get angry with my mom. She had enough rage for the entire family. But what I wouldn't do or say to my mom, I found myself doing and saying to Tom with a vengeance. We've noticed that many people do this. As we've said before, what was forbidden as a child is done to an extreme as an adult. My answer to Question #4 was "In my reactivity, I get angry and cry, accusing Tom of not caring for me and the girls, and then I withdraw and become the ice queen!" As you can see, there was no gentle, quiet spirit in this young wife! The amazing thing about the Digging Deeper exercise is that it helped me see what I actually *did* in conflict. Until that time, I would deny or defend my reactions, only focusing on Tom's offense. Question #4 really helps family members see and own what they do in conflict.

After you determine what you do, it is important to determine what you need to resolve the situation. This leads us to the next question.

Question #5: What do I really need?

This is where knowing what you need is essential. If you have trouble with this, use the list of basic needs you saw in chapter 13. We are looking for deeper needs, not just the things that will simply alleviate discomfort or pain. We want you to determine your soul needs. Before the Digging Deeper exercise, I would have said that what I needed was for Tom to simply come home earlier. This behavioral requirement would be met with his resistance, as he would provide a litany of reasons why he could not do what I had asked.

"I left the church late and traffic was a bear."

"Mr. Jones had gout and his family needed me to pray with him."

"I was doing hospital visits. Besides, it is my duty as a pastor to help others. Can't you see that?"

These defensive responses only inflamed my reactivity more. With the Digging Deeper exercise, I realized that what I really needed was *to feel safe*. As far back as I could remember I did not feel secure or protected. When my mom would be out late or my brother would bring his drug-addicted friends to the house in her absence, I felt terribly unsafe. These past soul wounds were triggered by Tom's actions. So after some deep pondering, my answer to Question #5 was *safety*.

Hearing this information enabled Tom to have empathy for me. Before that time he, like many people, would assume that I was simply being demanding or controlling, or just wanting my way. My requirement would surely create resistance from him. Now that he knew what had happened to me and why this need was so important, he was more able to have empathy. The compassion he felt for my childhood plight enabled Tom to move beyond his resistance and meet my need. The Digging Deeper exercise provided a paradigm shift for him to empathize with my pain and move toward healing it.

The wonderful thing about the Digging Deeper exercise is that now that we knew a basic need in my life that was not met, Tom could find ways to meet that need. Not only could he call when he was going to be late, he could also do other things to meet my safety need as well. These are called *healing behaviors*.

HEALING BEHAVIORS

When families do the Digging Deeper exercise, they are asked to list three things that they can do to meet the need of their loved one. These behaviors are powerful because they may seem like simple gestures but they can actually heal a wound deep in the soul. The loved one also provides three things that would heal his or her soul. Some of the behaviors on the two lists may even be the same things, making it easier.

In our Digging Deeper exercise the healing behaviors that I listed were:

- Call me regularly throughout the day and let me know when you think you will be arriving home.
- Put little notes around the house to let me know that I am important to you.
- Make sure the house is secure when we are home and away so that I feel safe.

Tom listed three things as well:

- I will get an alarm system for the house to make you feel safe.
- I will call whenever I can when I'm out.
- I will tell you how important you are to me daily and how I want you to feel safe with me.

Wow, I thought. *His list was even better than mine!* He committed to do these healing behaviors as much as he possibly could, and before I knew it, my soul began to heal. We now know that old-brain wounds are not healed as much by insight as by repetition. Tom's repeating these healing behaviors, because he could empathize with a little girl who did not feel safe healed my soul, and they can do the same for you.

THE SMITH FAMILY'S DIGGING DEEPER EXERCISE

After we taught Amy and Bill how to determine their needs, we had them invite the children into the counseling room so that we could teach them as well. We took a few minutes to explain the Digging Deeper exercise to them. Amy and Bill leaned forward in unison as they tried to catch every word we were saying. Chloe and Billy sat with their eyes fixed intently upon us. "Any questions before we start?" I asked. Chloe leaned over and whispered into her mom's ear. Mom listened and turned to me, hesitantly asking, "Chloe wants to share a trigger with her dad. Would that be okay?" We nodded in assent, knowing that in the past situations like this did not fare very well. It was our hope that the Digging Deeper exercise would make this time different.

Chloe's Question #1 (Trigger) "Dad," she began, "You have started to spend more time with me and Billy, and I really like it. You read to us, and take Bailey for walks, and have tickle fights, and I like all of these things. But when you go fishing with Uncle Bob and stay for days and days, I start to feel sad like I did when you did not spend time with us."

Before Chloe could identify her feelings in Question #2, Bill became defensive. "Chloe, I hardly ever go fishing anymore. I haven't been once this entire fall, and I didn't stay for days and days." Unfortunately, defensiveness and anger are common responses when we feel falsely accused or misunderstood. This is why staying with the format of the Digging Deeper exercise is so important.

"Hold on, Dad," Tom interrupted, trying to explain to Bill the futility of his behavior and get him back on track. "You don't have to defend yourself. You only have to listen. Chloe is not accusing you as much as telling you how she feels." Amy sat holding her breath, worried that what Chloe shared might upset Bill. But he soon calmed down and allowed Chloe to continue.

Chloe's Question #2 (Feeling) "Dad, when you go on a fishing trip I feel inferior, like I'm not important enough for you to stay home and be with me." By now, Bill was doing his best to practice mindfulness and intentionality, and really trying to *listen with agape* to Chloe. He sat quietly, showing as much empathy as he could.

Chloe's Question #3 (Past Occurrence) "I felt this before a lot in the past. Then I didn't feel it at all and that was awesome. But I guess now that you are changing, I think that I'm scared that it won't last and you'll go back to your old ways again."

"Great job getting in touch with your past like that, Chloe," I praised.

"This is a very normal fear for both children and adults," I explained to the family. "Once a person starts to change, the family can fear that it won't last." I then commended Bill for allowing Chloe to express her deep feelings.

"My dad would never let me tell him things like this when I was a kid," Bill interjected. "He would say that I was sassing or being disrespectful. You guys are helping me see that allowing my kids to tell me what is on their hearts, even when it is bad about me, is not disrespectful, it's honest!"

"Great insight," Tom added. "Bill, I can surely see how the Lord is changing you."

Chloe continued.

Chloe's Question #4 (Reaction) "When this happens, I react by crying and not wanting to talk to you." (It seemed that Chloe had learned the same stonewalling technique that Mom and Dad used with each other.)

Chloe's Question #5 (Need) "At first I thought that I needed you never to go fishing again. But now that I'm saying this to you, I can see that it probably wouldn't be fair. I would not want you to tell me that I couldn't go to Mandy's house for sleepovers ever again." (Often this happens with the Digging Deeper exercise. Once a person gets to say what they need without being interrupted or shut down, they realize that the need may be extreme and should be altered and amended to something more fair and realistic.)

We praised Chloe for her astute realization and instructed her to look at the needs list in order to determine a more realistic idea of what she needed. Chloe continued, "So, I guess what I need is to know that you still want to be with me, even though you go fishing sometimes." Chloe then looked at the list saying, "Let's see, my need would be—

connection. Oh, and I need to feel like I am special to you. That would be signi . . . fi . . . cance." Chloe had a little trouble pronouncing it and Bill helped her. We could hear the empathy in his voice and we could see that he was actually getting what Chloe was saying.

Chloe did an excellent job of determining what she needed, and with a little coaching, Bill did an excellent job of listening to her. By not getting defensive or angry, he could hear what was on Chloe's heart and have empathy for her. All she wanted was for him to quell her fear that the old Dad would come back. Once Bill realized this, he had no need for anger. In fact, he also realized that this was what Amy had been trying to tell him about Chloe for some time, but his defensiveness got in the way of his hearing effectively. After realizing this, Bill was ready to respond to Chloe.

Bill leaned over, lowering his head, trying to get down to Chloe's level. He looked at her intently as he spoke softly to Chloe and said, "Honey, now that you've told me how you feel, I finally get what you have been trying to say to me. I want you to know that you are important to me and my going fishing does not take away from that. I try to show you, but I guess you need more. What can I do to help you see that you are special to me?"

Chloe grinned from ear to ear. "Great job," I broke in. "When you don't know how to meet the needs of a family member, instead of getting defensive or giving up, asking a question is an excellent way of finding out what you can do to help." We then instructed both Chloe and Bill to come up with at least three healing behaviors that would meet Chloe's need to feel connected and special.

Chloe had a little trouble determining some healing behaviors, so Bill volunteered. "Three things that I can do to heal Chloe's soul wounds are:

1. Take you along on a fishing trip, just you and me.

2. Read with you as much as I can when I'm not on the road to show you that you are special.

3. Tell you how much you mean to me as often as I can."

These were huge behaviors for a man who could not get in touch with his emotions when he first came to counseling. Chloe's whole body seemed to smile at his suggestions. "Dad, yours are better than anything I could have listed," she squealed with delight. She only had one to add to his list. "I want Dad to help me train Bailey to do tricks." Chloe had tried to train this mongrel for some time and she wanted Dad to supervise.

Even though Bill didn't enjoy training a hyperactive puppy, he knew how much it meant to Chloe, so he gladly agreed. He then added, "Chloe, I understand how you could be afraid that the old dad would return, especially if I get mad at you for bringing up my old ways. You don't have to be scared that the old dad will come back. I don't want to ever be that guy again, and I will work hard to make sure of that. I'm sorry that I spent so much time away from you and Billy. I learned a lot of bad habits from my family and I sure don't want to pass them on to you two."

At this point Bill and Amy were crying. Tears glistened in Chloe's eyes as she spontaneously came over and sat on her dad's knee. She put her thin arms around his big neck and cried tears of joy. As Bill continued, he reached for Billy and pulled him on his other knee. It was an awesome sight, seeing this big bear of a man cuddling two kids on his lap.

Softly he said, "I want you both to know that you are very important to me and I want you to grow up knowing this. I love you two very much and I will do what I can to be a good dad, a loving dad, a dad that heals instead of wounds."

These are the moments that Tom and I live for and we believe that this is why God put us on this earth. Tom and I have often said that we want to take our last breath watching a family move from withholding to giving, from resentment to empathy, and from wounding to healing.

The Digging Deeper exercise helped the Smith family overcome their resistance to requirement, learn what their needs were, and develop empathy for one another. It can do the same thing for you and your family.

Healing Homework

- ~ As a family, have each member identify what their greatest needs are. You may use the needs in chapter 13.
- ~ Make a list of at least three healing behaviors that each of you can do to meet those needs.
- ~ Practice the Digging Deeper exercise when you have triggers that need deep-rooted healing.
- ~ Lastly, shower the people you love with love. It is never too late to have or make a happy childhood.

God's Design for
a Healthy Family

You may be asking as you read this book, "How does the Smith family's healing process apply to me?" You might say, "Our situation is different. Our problems are deeper and more damaging than anything the Smiths ever faced. They still had hope that things could be better. Our family is too wounded and we've hurt one another much more than they ever did. We've gone too far. . . ."

We hear people say things like this quite often in our office. But what they say is not true. There is hope. You can change. No matter what has happened, what you have done, what you have said to hurt one another, there is always hope that you can change. The change that comes with the Soul-Healing Love of Christ is not limited by the depth and extent that you have hurt one another. It is much more about the degree of your willingness to face the hurts, to understand and communicate about them with each other, and to apply the very same healing tools and techniques the Smiths used to your family.

The only thing that will cause you not to change your family forever is your fear, which can lead to an unwillingness to try. The tools of Soul-Healing Love are not magical, but they are powerful and transforming when you are willing to apply them to your hurting family situation. Remember the old southern saying: "If you keep doing what you have always done, you will keep gettin' what you have always got."

As you read about God's design for any healthy family, please summon the courage to try these techniques yourself, and with your family. You have very little to lose and a great deal of healing and transformation to gain. We know from decades of experience working with families like the Smiths that if you try, it will work for you, too. God bless you richly and deeply on this healing journey.

THE REST OF THE SMITHS' STORY

We saw the Smiths a few more times before they "graduated." (Most family therapists call this termination, but we prefer graduation.) We followed up after three months, just to make sure that they were doing their Healing Homework. In one of the last sessions, I asked them what they had learned from their soul-healing journey.

Both Amy and Bill said that learning about and experiencing the unconditional love of Christ was life-changing for them. "I always knew in my head that God loved me," Bill answered. "At least that's what the priests and nuns always taught us. But now I know it in my heart."

Tom and I have used this model with thousands of families over the years, and even with us God's unconditional love that heals our souls is still sinking in. The love of God is unfathomable, yet glorious.

Amy said, "We have also learned some great communication tools to use to get us out of our power struggles."

Bill added, "One thing I learned was that I'm not a monster. Really, my anger and withdrawal made me think that there was something wrong with me. Now I know that it is reactivity and I can do something about it. I can, unlike my dad, control my anger with the Lord's help."

"We learned what was underneath our anger," Billy chirped, as he put up four fingers naming all of the primary emotions—guilt, inferiority, fear, and trauma. He then proceeded to squirm in his seat and kick his legs out in front of him as an expression of accomplishment. Of course Chloe, not to be outdone, offered, "We learned to put ourselves in each other's shoes and have empathy for one another."

Bill then looked at us with his big piercing eyes and said, "I think that I learned more than anybody. I saw how much I had hurt my family and didn't even know it. Having empathy for them has really humbled me and brought about a lot of repentance and forgiveness for our whole family."

Perhaps the greatest gem came from little six-year-old Billy who had been a trouper for months in family therapy. He leaned forward, grinning, as the billowy cushions of the couch enveloped him. He was obviously eager to answer and best his sister. "I know, I know, Dr. Bev!" he yelled. "I learned that Jesus loves us, Dad loves Mom, Dad loves us, and we all love each other. And that's what family is all about. You can't get any better than that."

And he was right. Who could?!

Glossary

Adaptations—behavior patterns that we develop in order to cope with the unhealthy messages of the soul wounds that we incurred early in life. Adaptations reinforce these messages, rather than heal them.

Alliance of Lies—a set of agreements we make with the enemy of our souls, in believing, accepting, and living by the messages of our soul wounds.

Agape love—love that is unearned and given unconditionally to us by God first, and then freely given to one another in response to His great love for us.

Caretaking—unhealthy sacrificial love, care, and devotion one gives to another in order to feel some sense of self-worth. It generates a false sense of self-esteem.

Divine destiny—being set apart for a specific and divine purpose. The call of God on one's life.

Divine oneness—the sense of fullness and completion achieved by coupling a man (God's male-likeness) and a woman (God's female-likeness) together, and most completely replicate both sides of God.

Divine Us—the divine call on the life of a couple that can only be achieved by the synergy created in divine oneness. This generates a level of performance that neither could achieve on his or her own.

Enmeshment—a state of false intimacy created by a parent toward his or her child when that parent confides in, shares emotionally with, and in some cases actually creates a surrogate relationship with that child, becoming too close to the child in that relationship, and taking away his or her need for autonomy and independence.

Externalize—the tendency to deal with one's emotions by outwardly expressing them rather than holding them in.

Family dysfunction—unhealthy patterns of thinking, feeling, and acting that wound family members and create unhealthy situations and behaviors.

Family of origin—the family in which an individual grew up during their formative years, consisting of parents, siblings, and extended family members.

Generational transmission of dysfunction—the tendency to pass down to future generations the unhealthy behavior patterns, characteristics, and traits of family members who came before.

Habituation—the tendency to use adaptive behaviors so regularly and commonly that they become unconscious habits.

Healing behaviors—a set of simple yet completely targeted behaviors that one does for another to meet that individual's most basic needs, potentially healing their soul wounds.

Hurling or hiding—adaptive behaviors that individuals use in an attempt to deal with their deep inner emotions. Hurlers project those feelings onto others while hiders internalize those emotions, pushing them into their unconscious minds.

Indulgences—unhealthy behaviors that people allow themselves when adaptations no longer work. Addictions are the most common form of indulgences, and these behaviors generally reinforce the wounds, fear, guilt, and shame we feel rather than resolving them.

Intentionality—the willingness to treat people in a way that heals, no matter how we feel emotionally.

Interactivity—when one person in a relationship triggers the other's basic fears and taps into wounds while simultaneously being triggered as well. In that moment, both people are triggered and both are reacting to those triggers.

Internalize—to allow the messages of one's soul wounds to define oneself (i.e., to believe, contrary to evidence, that I am a failure, I am unlovable, that something is wrong with me).

Love cocktail—term coined by University of New York researchers used to describe the various chemicals within the brain that are released when a person "falls in love." (i.e., dopamine, epinephrine, norepinephrine, phenylethylamine, etc.).

Marital Pac-Man—a term used in the Soul-Healing Love model to describe the basic pursuer/distancer dyad that is created by one partner pursuing the other in a relationship while the other partner distances or moves away from that relationship.

Marital purgatory—a desperate dilemma that couples get into when the behaviors and actions of each person create further distance between them rather than creating intimacy.

Mindfulness—the state of being aware and attentive to your own soul wounds, as well as to the soul wounds of your family members.

Narcissism—the tendency to become hyper self-focused, thinking only of oneself, rather than the desires and needs of others.

Neurobiology—the study of the brain, its chemical makeup, and its various functions.

Old brain—the cerebellum, or primitive brain; the storehouse of traumatic memories. This is also the location of the autonomic nervous system, which produces a basic fight-or-flight response to potential or perceived danger.

Ownership—the conscious decision of a person's will to "own" and understand the part he/she plays in conflicts, rather than projecting blame onto the other person.

Parentified child—a phenomenon that occurs in dysfunctional family systems whereby children are required to assume the roles and behaviors of more mature adults and denied the opportunity to behave as children.

Phenomenon of recognition—the tendency to be drawn to or attracted to people who have similar soul wounds from the past. We feel very comfortable and familiar with that person even though we may have just met him or her.

Power struggle—when each person in a relationship wants his own way and struggles to get it while at the same time resisting others. There is an underlying tension that is always there, whether one is aware of it or not. It is characterized by fear and causes a breakdown in communication, which leads to assumptions. In a power struggle, a person always assumes the worst and projects it onto their mate or other family members.

Reactivity—the tendency to give a situation more emotional energy or a bigger reaction than it deserves, because a soul wound has been impacted.

Renounce—to repudiate, disown, and turn away from unhealthy beliefs, thoughts, and ideas.

Shut-down response—the tendency to become frozen emotionally, verbally, or physically when confronted in a relationship.

Similar wounds/opposite adaptations—the unconscious tendency for people to be drawn to others who have very similar soul wounds, but opposite ways of dealing with those soul wounds; opposites attract even unconsciously.

Soul-Healing Love—the model of relationships developed by Drs. Bev and Tom Rodgers that provides ways for couples and family members to be healing agents to each others' deepest wounds and to sacrifice in relationships by following Christ's example of agape. It helps people move from inadvertently wounding each other to consciously healing each other with the Lord's inspiration and help.

Soul wound—a basic need that was not met, usually in childhood, that impacts the soul of a person. It then defines who that person is, and how he or she will react to others in his or her environment and in relationships.

Triggers—events, situations, or actions that occur in relationships that impact soul wounds from one's past.

Notes

Chapter 1

1. Anastasia Toufexis, "The Right Chemistry" (*Time Magazine*, February 15, 1993), 48–49.
2. Pat Love, EdD, *The Truth About Love* (New York: Simon & Schuster, 2001), 153.
3. Harville Hendrix, *Keeping the Love You Find* (New York: Pocket Books, 1992), 217.
4. John Gottman, *The Marriage Clinic* (New York: Norton & Norton, 1999), 229.

Chapter 3

1. Harville Hendrix, *Keeping the Love You Find,* 40–41.
2. Murray Bowen, *Family Therapy and Clinical Practice* (New York: J. Aronson, 1978).

Chapter 4

1. Paula Rinehart, *Perfect Every Time,* (Colorado Springs: NavPress, 1992), 149–150.

Chapter 5

1. James Dobson, *Parenting Isn't for Cowards,* (Waco: Word Publishing, 1987), 205.

Chapter 7

1. Gottman, *The Marriage Clinic,* 41–46.
2. Rodgers, *Adult Children of Divorced Parents,* 55.

3. Toufexis, "The Right Chemistry," 48.
4. Scott Stanley and Howard Markman, *Marriage in the 90s: A National Random Phone Survey* (Denver: Prep Inc, 1997), as quoted on http://www.smartmarriages.com/7.html.

Chapter 9

1. David Seamands, *Healing for Damaged Emotions* (Wheaton: Victor Books, 1981).

Chapter 10

1. Tim Clinton, Ed Hindson, George Ohlschlager, *The Soul Care Bible* (Nashville: Thomas Nelson, 2001), 883.

Chapter 11

1. http://barna.org/FlexPage.aspx?Page=BarnaUpdate&Barna UpdateID=295
2. Centers for Disease Control, "Cohabitation, Marriage, Divorce, and Remarriage in the United States" 23 (22) (Hyattsville, MD: Department of Health and Human Services, 2002), 2, or http://www.cdc.gov/nchs/data/series/sr_23/sr23_022.pdf.

Chapter 13

1. Gottman, *The Marriage Clinic*, 193–94, 226.

Chapter 14

1. Gottman, *The Marriage Clinic*, 168.

About the Authors

Beverly and Tom Rodgers hold PhDs in clinical Christian counseling and have owned and operated Rodgers Christian Counseling in Charlotte, North Carolina, for the past 28 years. There they have a clinic with seven therapists who see an average of 150 patients per week. Ten years ago they started the Institute for Soul-Healing Love, a training facility for pastors, interns, counselors, mentors, and lay leaders, where they teach their Soul-Healing Love Model.

Dr. Beverly also holds a master's degree in marital and family therapy from Northern Illinois University and is a licensed marriage and family therapist. Dr. Tom has a master's degree in counseling from Azusa Pacific University, and another master's degree from the University of North Carolina, and he is a licensed professional counselor. Both are members of many professional organizations including Association for Marriage and Family Ministries, American Association of Christian Counselors, and American Association of Marital and Family Therapy, among others. Bev and Tom are the authors of *Soul-Healing Love: Turning Relationships That Hurt Into Relationships That Heal, How to Find Mr. or Ms. Right: A Practical Guide to Finding a Soul Mate, Adult Children of Divorced Parents: Making Your Marriage Work*, and *The Singlehood Phenomenon: 10 Brutally Honest Reasons People Aren't Getting Married*.

Bev and Tom have been married for more than 32 years and have two grown daughters.

FOCUS ON THE FAMILY®

Welcome to the Family

Whether you purchased this book, borrowed it, or received it as a gift, we're glad you're reading it. It's just one of the many helpful, encouraging, and biblically based resources produced by Focus on the Family® for people in all stages of life.

Focus began in 1977 with the vision of one man, Dr. James Dobson, a licensed psychologist and author of numerous best-selling books on marriage, parenting, and family. Alarmed by the societal, political, and economic pressures that were threatening the existence of the American family, Dr. Dobson founded Focus on the Family with one employee and a once-a-week radio broadcast aired on 36 stations.

Now an international organization reaching millions of people daily, Focus on the Family is dedicated to preserving values and strengthening and encouraging families through the life-changing message of Jesus Christ.

Focus on the Family MAGAZINES

These faith-building, character-developing publications address the interests, issues, concerns, and challenges faced by every member of your family from preschool through the senior years.

For More INFORMATION

ONLINE:
Log on to
FocusOnTheFamily.com
In Canada, log on to
FocusOnTheFamily.ca

PHONE:
Call toll-free:
800-A-FAMILY
(232-6459)
In Canada, call toll-free:
800-661-9800

FOCUS ON
THE FAMILY
MAGAZINE

FOCUS ON
THE FAMILY
CLUBHOUSE JR.™
Ages 4 to 8

FOCUS ON
THE FAMILY
CLUBHOUSE®
Ages 8 to 12

FOCUS ON
THE FAMILY
CITIZEN®
U.S. news issues

Rev. 12/08

More Great Resources
from Focus on the Family®

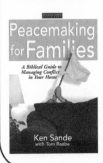

The Institute for Soul Healing Love

Soul healing love is a model of counseling and relationships developed by Drs. Bev and Tom Rodgers that integrates principles of psychological health with biblical truth. No one can go through life without sustaining wounds. Soul Healing Love helps individuals and families heal those wounds with the help of God's unconditional love. It does this by teaching practical, easy-to-learn communication tools and techniques designed to manage anger, resolve conflict, solve problems, and reconcile differences. You will gain awareness, enhance empathy, foster forgiveness, and turn hurting moments into healing moments in your relationships.

The Institute for Soul Healing Love was established by Drs. Bev and Tom Rodgers as an offshoot of Rodgers Christian Counseling in Charlotte, NC. Through it they have trained 500 counselors, pastors, lay leaders, and mentors in 27 states, the Bahamas, South Korea, and Singapore. The Rodgerses have developed books, workbooks, DVDs, and training manuals to help participants and leaders use the model effectively.

Drs. Bev and Tom conduct workshops for singles, couples, and families covering a variety of topics.

Contact information:
704 281-1754
www.soulhealinglove.com
adultchildrenofdivorcedparents.com
becomingafamilythatheals.com